THE
ARCHERS
in Fact
and Fiction

THE
ARCHERS
in Fact
and Fiction

Academic Analyses of
Life in Rural Borsetshire

Edited by **Cara Courage, Nicola Headlam**
and **Peter Matthews**

PETER LANG

Oxford • Bern • Berlin • Bruxelles • Frankfurt am Main • New York • Wien

Bibliographic information published by Die Deutsche Nationalbibliothek.
Die Deutsche Nationalbibliothek lists this publication in the Deutsche National-
bibliografie; detailed bibliographic data is available on the Internet at
http://dnb.d-nb.de.

A catalogue record for this book is available from the British Library.

Library of Congress Control Number: 2016959089

"The Archers" and "BBC Radio 4" are trademarks of the British Broadcasting
Corporation and are used under licence.

Cover image: Singularity © Finn Hopson.

ISBN 978-1-78707-119-3 (print) • ISBN 978-1-78707-120-9 (ePDF)
ISBN 978-1-78707-305-0 (ePub) • ISBN 978-1-78707-306-7 (mobi)

© Peter Lang AG 2017

Published by Peter Lang Ltd, International Academic Publishers,
52 St Giles, Oxford, OX1 3LU, United Kingdom
oxford@peterlang.com, www.peterlang.com

This publication has been peer reviewed.

Printed in Germany

Contents

vi

Figures

CARA COURAGE, NICOLA HEADLAM AND PETER MATTHEWS

Introduction to *Academic Archers*: The Birth of a New Academic Community

On Wednesday 17 February 2016, around one hundred people met in a lecture theatre in central London for an academic seminar with a difference. The first difference was that most of the day was spent laughing uproariously. The second difference was the conference stopped at 2pm to listen to the broadcast of *The Archers* – the world's longest-running soap opera – on BBC Radio 4. In fact the whole day was devoted to this 'everyday story of country folk', or the 'contemporary drama in a rural setting' as it is more recently described.

The seminar came about from a discussion on Twitter between the three editors of this volume. We became linked through our shared research interest in something very un-Ambridge: urban research and urbanism. During the tense early days of the planning of Route B and the *Save the Am Vale Environment* campaign (see the chapters by Chris Perkins and Peter Matthews), through brief exchanges we realized that we could either use our academic research to illuminate issues in *The Archers* or use *The Archers* storylines to make our research more accessible.

All three editors have long histories with *The Archers*. Cara Courage had *The Archers* forced upon her as a child in her grandmother's farm kitchen, finding it terminally boring and resenting having to be quiet when it was on and having to listen to all the boring farming talk spoken by these boring adults. She returned to it in her thirties, out of sheer laziness to rush to the radio turn it off when it came on, as so many (astoundingly) do. Thus *The Archers* crept back in her life through an aural osmosis. Nicola Headlam, sharing a birthday with the dreadful Kate Madikane (*née* Archer), had followed her teenage dramas with interest but dropped out of active listenership from the mid-1990s to the mid-2000s. She picked up again when doctoral study meant a lot of working from home with the radio on. Peter Matthews briefly listened when Adam and Ian clinched in the polytunnel, amazed that such a typically English programme could feature a same-sex relationship so prominently. Alas the Brian/Siobhán storyline was too much for an impressionable twenty-one-year-old. A few years later he was dating a chorister who was in church every Sunday morning and as the BBC Radio 4 schedule segued into the omnibus, the storylines began to stick, and the rest is history.

After arranging the practicalities (we tried to hire Lower Loxley Hall or Grey Gables as the venue, but even though it was the Borsetshire quiet season, they were both, mysteriously, hard to get hold of) the call for papers for a seminar was announced in autumn 2015. We were absolutely overwhelmed by the response – although as the chapter by Lyn Thomas highlights, we should not have been surprised. Academics are the archetypal demographic of an *Archers* listener. As Peter is at the University of Stirling, we were quite surprised not to get a submission from one of its former faculty members, Professor Jim Lloyd. After pulling some strings with his colleagues in the History Department, we did manage to get him to review Philippa Byrne's and Samantha Walton's contributions to this volume. We'll leave it up to the reader to decide whether this was a wise decision. After a rigorous review process the thirteen papers that now form this volume were selected. Of course tickets for the event sold out in hours as *Archers* fans pressed to attend.

A theme running throughout the day, and throughout the chapters below, is the blurring between the lines of fact and fiction in interpretations of life in Ambridge. The audience, and speakers, could barely keep a straight face as academics pondered why Borsetshire County Council did not respond to a Freedom of Information request regarding care home fees (made by Jo Moriarty), why Pip Archer had seemingly undergone a laryngeal transplant in her brief trip to Yorkshire (observed by William Barras), or why the General Medical Council had not long ago struck off Dr Richard Locke (raised by Deborah Bowman). Carenza Lewis and Clemency Cooper fully immersed themselves in Borsetshire by imagining how the residents of Ambridge would respond to community archaeology in the village. In keeping with academic protocol, the chapters in this book are all 'peer-reviewed' by an *Archers* character.

Famously, *The Archers* keeps a substantial archive to make sure that storylines that have run for up to sixty years are consistent. However, further hilarity was caused by the inconsistencies that slip-in: that Ruth and David Archer seemed to forget they had a bedroom in Bridge Farm where Ruth's mother could stay; the ever-changing route of the River Am analysed from the perspective of human geography (by Chris Perkins); or the mysterious disappearance of a home for disabled children sometime in the 1980s (noted by Katherine Runswick-Cole).

It was actually the accuracy of *The Archers* storylines that provided the main contents for the papers and the chapters in this volume. That the scripts have parallels to great works of drama – such as *Othello* – provided an analogy for Abi Pattenden; the themes of ecology and evoking a sense of the countryside against encroaching modernism provided inspiration for Philippa Byrne and Samantha Walton. Issues of country life such as industrial injuries in agriculture (covered by Neil Mansfield and Lauren Morgan), social care for older people (Jo Moriarty), affordable housing provision and development (Peter Matthews), and the ethics of assisted suicide (Deborah Bowman) were all so accurately and movingly portrayed by the programme that storylines became the subjects of academic analysis. Katherine Runswick-Cole's chapter, however, highlights a major omission from *The Archers* over the years – disabled people who are removed through 'narrative prosthesis'.

The seminar occurred during the height of Rob Titchener's campaign of coercive control over his wife Helen. As reported later, the research with domestic violence charities that the production team and actors had done made this so realistic that Helen M. Burrows could describe how she applies it in educating the next generation of social workers that might help the Helen, Henry and Jack Titcheners of the country. The seminar was proud also to add to the financial donations for domestic violence charities that flooded in due to the storyline.

The attention to detail of the *Archers* production team then is matched by the attention to academic detail of the authors in this edited collection. However, we know it will not meet the attention to detail of the avid fans of *The Archers*, something we were all taken aback with on the day. Facing a learned and esteemed conference audience, it is not often – or ever – that you will hear the speaker apologize for being wet behind the ears in their subject after only fifteen years of study, yet, with 'listener-academics' in the room with whole lifetimes of active research in the programme, we were but mere apprentices. So, please forgive any omissions or errors. We present this edited collection as, first, a reflection of our mutual love of this continuing drama that seems quintessentially part of Britain, and second, as a way to reveal new insights into *The Archers* and new ways to enjoy the programme. Finally the volume aims to bring the excellent research that is carried out in our universities to a wider audience. A Facebook group has been formed, *Academic Archers*, to continue the conversation long after the day. This was the first *Academic Archers* conference, but we certainly hope it will not be the last.

LYN THOMAS

The Archers and its Listeners in the Twenty-First Century: Drama, Nostalgia and the Rural Everyday

In his 2013 book Radio in the Digital Age, *Andrew Dubber (2013: 6) reflects on the difficulty of defining the specific characteristics of radio, and presents his project as being 'about radio and everything radio means – in an age characterized by digital media'. This formulation is useful as a way of approaching* The Archers *in the twenty-first century. What I am going to discuss in this chapter is not just the radio broadcast, or even the technological advances that make it possible to listen to the programme online at a time of your choosing, but the cultural spaces of communication that have evolved and are constantly evolving around the programme. I will be looking both at the programme and the way people talk about it on and offline and the cultural resources they draw on and create in so doing. I will refer to my earlier phases of research on the programme and its listeners – the first, in the late 1990s, and the second in 2007–8 as well as the present moment – in order to explore how* The Archers, *defined in this broad sense, has evolved since the late twentieth century, and is evolving in the twenty-first. A striking aspect of this evolution is the changing relationship between listeners and programme-makers – scriptwriters, producers and actors – and this will also be one of the strands of my discussion here.*

In my title I have highlighted a set of themes or discourses which seem to me to characterize the cultural phenomenon that is *The Archers*. Like other soap operas *The Archers* relies, and always has relied on, a strong narrative drive to hold its listeners. But unlike most other soaps its original mission was didactic – the programme was designed to help farmers increase yields and improve practices in the post-war period, when food production was a high national priority. Since its inception *The Archers* has retained this commitment to the representation of rural life, and particularly the challenges and dilemmas facing farmers. The latter can of course become dramatic storylines, but *The Archers* has always included scenes of everyday activities on the farms, and more broadly in the village, creating a sense, alongside the drama, of the continuity of life in a quiet Borsetshire backwater. Comedy and light relief have also always been woven in – the trials and tribulations of Lynda Snell's annual theatre productions, Jennifer's new kitchen and canapé recipes or the Grundys' money-making schemes and cider club antics. Within the programme there is a constant reworking of the balance between these elements, and in talk about the programme listeners are often torn between attachment to the everyday story and the desire for compelling drama.

These tensions are heightened by the fact that the programme's longevity and the rural setting have given *The Archers* a special status in the construction of a pastoral vision of Englishness, still a dominant trope in national identity, despite the lack of fit with the realities of multi-ethnic, multicultural Britain. In his chapter in Robert Colls and Philip Dodd's recently re-published collection on *Englishness, Politics and Culture*, Alun Howkins demonstrates how Englishness was culturally connected with rurality in the late nineteenth and early twentieth centuries; in his examination of the literary and musical culture of the time he describes an ideological move away from the England of self-made men and dark satanic mills to the dream of the 'South Country', where in contrast to the cities,

> men and women still live naturally. The air is clean, personal relationships matter (especially between employer and employee), there is no crime (except 'quaint' crime like poaching) and no violence. It is an organic society, a 'real' one, as opposed to the unnatural or 'unreal' society of the town. (Howkins in Colls and Dodd [1986] 2014: 86)

I would argue that in the post-war period *The Archers* has continued this ideological work, placing the 'South Country', which can be stretched to the South Midlands, though not, Howkins argues, to Cornwall or East Anglia, at the heart of national identity.

Interestingly, in his interview on the sixty-fifth anniversary broadcast the editor of *The Archers* at the time, Sean O'Connor, made exactly this kind of claim for the programme's significance: 'It's perhaps about who we used to be as a nation, who we are now, and where we think we're going'. In this interview he also makes a new pact with the audience, a twenty-first-century mission statement, pledging to take the programme back to its essence, that is, 'essentially a show about farming', and implying that he will not indulge in the dramatic excesses of the previous regime, or repeat the mistakes of the sixtieth anniversary broadcast. This time, no one was going to fall off a roof or undergo an emergency Caesarean; it would just be the family round the table, talking about the future of the dairy herd. Jill Archer, whose voice epitomizes continuity more than any other, and who has been doling out sympathy, tea, cake and casseroles for almost sixty years, was given a key line: 'I think I'll make coffee and I'm sure we could all do with a piece of fruitcake.' Among the many tweets mocking the lack of excitement in the anniversary episode were those who loved Patricia Greene's 1940s articulation of the word fruitcake: 'Jill must be the only person who could quell a revolution with a firmly worded offer of fruitcake'; 'Jill's best line all year – "Fruitcake" – worthy of the Royal Shakespeare Company'. The 'back to the old days' feeling of the episode was also praised by some listener-tweeters: 'four voices, tea and fruitcake in the farmhouse kitchen and a proper discussion about the cows. ... Ah just like #thearchers used to be ...'. So what are the elements that make up Ambridge past, that some listeners are so attached to, or at least declaring attachment to?

In my discussion of *The Archers* in *Fans, Feminisms and 'Quality' Media*, I read the radio serial through critical work on literary adaptations on TV and film, such as *A Room with a View* or *Howards End*. In his work on British heritage films of the 1980s film scholar Andrew Higson developed the notion of heritage space, arguing that there is an emphasis on spectacle, rather than narrative in these films – where the camera lingers on carefully crafted period details of clothing, furniture, architecture and landscape (Thomas 2002; Higson 1993). In *The Archers* something equivalent to this is created through sound. The fictional space of the village and its environs is evoked through sound effects and dialogue based on a range of precise locations and the relationships between them, so that listeners acquire their own personal sense of the geography of Ambridge. The fact that most of the villagers live in picturesquely named cottages (Glebe, Honeysuckle, April, Keeper's and so on), farmhouses, substantial country dwellings such as Ambridge Hall or the Dower House, or even in the actual mansions Lower Loxley or Grey Gables contributes to the 'picture postcard in sound' effect. Lower Loxley, with its Tree Top Walk and seasonal events offers an auditory version of the experience of the countryside doubtless shared by many of the listeners – the day out at a National Trust property – nicely finished off by tea in The Orangery.

Dialogues occasionally contain descriptions of the beautiful rural surroundings enjoyed by the characters, which temporarily suspend the narrative and invite the listener to imagine the scene, just as lingering shots of parks and countryside provide moments of spectacle in the heritage film. Lakey Hill, complete with whistling wind, trudging footsteps and birdsong, has often been the scene of moments of reflection, philosophical wisdom or intense emotion. On 1 May 2011 Kenton and Jolene reflected on their holiday in Monte Carlo during a walk on Lakey Hill, reaffirming their bonds with Ambridge during the walk, with Jolene commenting on the beauties of new leaves and hawthorn blossom as they look down on the village. More recently David and Ruth contemplated the new plans for Brookfield (and Jill slaving away in the kitchen) from the heights of Lakey Hill. Lilian and Justin Elliott made a foray to the same location, conversing on the perhaps more mundane topic of local property prices, but at the same time emphasizing Lilian's country woman heritage – even if Lilian is really more 'silver stilettos' than 'tweed and headscarf'. We might prefer to draw a veil over Pip's romantic trysts with Matthew in the same location ...

The heritage space of Ambridge also has a temporal dimension in that seasonal patterns of English rural life are observed. As Christine Geraghty (1991: 87) has argued in relation to British television soaps, rituals of this kind are used to bring the community together in one space, and to represent it symbolically. However, in the case of *The Archers*, the rural setting gives a particular heritage twist to these moments of bonding. *The Archers* may be listened to by city dwellers, for whom November and February may not seem very different, but the programmes depict a world where changes of season are fundamental aspects of individual experience, and social and working life. Every spring we visit the lambing shed, while most summers feature a cricket story and/or a village fête, followed in the autumn by the Flower and Produce Show, Bonfire Night and the Christmas lights. In 2015, very much in this tradition, wassailing was introduced for the first time, and were it not for *The Archers*, would we still know about Stir-Up

Sunday? The effect of this revival of the calendar of traditional rural life is the same kind of construction of nostalgic Englishness that we find in *Downton Abbey* and other heritage texts.

In both phases of my research on *The Archers* respondents have commented on the pleasures afforded by these aspects of the programme – the rural heritage space it allows them to imagine, and the narrative's quieter moments:

> I close my eyes while listening and I am in a country pub, a farmhouse kitchen or feeding ducks on the village green. (Female, 50s, retired registrar, questionnaire, 1997)

> News of farming and rural life, interested in the story. Have got to know the characters over the years. (Female, 40s, local government officer, questionnaire, 2008)

> Actually they are all dull but that's what I like about it. It is quite soothing to hear Ruth and David mithering on about badgers on a Sunday morning. I hate it when it gets all sensational. (Mumsnet, 8 January 2008)

This last quotation exemplifies the role ascribed to *The Archers* by many listeners: a reassuring presence in the background of their lives. This desire for stability and 'mithering on about badgers', cows, hens and so on recurs in talk about the programme, even if the more dramatic storylines sometimes improve the ratings.

This role as comforting background to, or distraction from, everyday activities is intensified by the personally nostalgic dimension of a programme some listeners have accompanied since its first broadcast in 1951, and many have listened to for several decades. Attachment to Ambridge past is connected with memories of childhood and of home, so that the remaining familiar voices and theme tune can have a comforting effect:

> I've listened ever since I was a child. My mother was a great fan of the programme so it was always on at 7 o'clock in the evening. So it was just always there, it seeped into my radio listening at a very early age. Of course as you grow up with the programme you get to know who the characters are. It was rather nice and reassuring. It was always on at the same time each day. It was always on in the kitchen at home so I tended to associate it with home cooking rather so it was rather pleasant oral wallpaper rather than the drama but when I grew up I started being interested in the characters a bit more. (Male, 30s, university lecturer, interview, 2008)

The utopian qualities of the Ambridge community are also an important aspect of this nostalgic relationship to the programme, and Alun Howkins's comment on the imagining of rural England as a place where 'personal relationships matter' fits Ambridge well. Christine Geraghty argues that setting is the basis of the soap opera community; in relation to stereotypical representations of cockneys and northerners she comments: 'What is significant is that soaps have used such assumptions as a means of presenting the viewer with a community in which difference from outsiders is asserted not by money or ambition or power but by qualities which can be shared by virtue of living in the same place' (Geraghty 1991: 92). The sense of place created by the textual features enumerated above similarly contributes to the construction of the ideal community in *The Archers*. Travel outside the boundaries of Borsetshire at times seems to carry an inherent threat – 'Cumbria of all places' to quote Pip Archer commenting on Matthew's departure for northern climes – to say nothing of the dangers of motorway service stations. However, culturally and socially disparate characters within those boundaries share an extraordinary level of communication and communion. Whilst this level of communication is clearly necessary to the soap opera genre, the effect is nonetheless a representation of a closely knit community, or what would now be called 'social cohesion'. After the controversial and sudden death in a car crash of Mark Hebden, the village rallied round to support his widow Shula and she reciprocated by presenting a trophy in memory of Mark to the cricket club. Thus this 'tragedy', which heightened the emotional intensity of a fictional world based at that time largely on the 'everyday', was woven back into the succession of community events, the calendar of village life. After the flood of March 2015 we found luxury hotel Grey Gables offering rooms to homeless villagers on a surprisingly long-term basis – the Grundys only left just before Christmas – and were again rescued from exile from Ambridge by Caroline and Oliver Sterling. Only in Ambridge would an upper-middle-class couple spending the winter in Tuscany offer their boutiqued farmhouse home to a working-class family whose older generation male protagonists are not always on the right side of the law.

The boundaries of the utopia are nonetheless demarcated in terms of race and ethnicity. The issue of rural racism was foregrounded in a story about a racist attack by Roy Tucker and other youths on lawyer Usha Gupta in her early days in Ambridge. Since then Usha has become fully integrated into the village community, but when Usha married the vicar, Alan Franks, Shula found this so difficult that she transferred her allegiance and attendance to Felpersham Cathedral. In this case, the scripts seemed to be problematizing the utopian community and idealized vision of England and Englishness that I have discussed. It was, I would argue, a significant moment for *The Archers*. In recent storylines Usha and Alan, and his mixed-race daughter Amy, have almost disappeared from the scripts, despite the obvious relevance their roles as lawyer, vicar and midwife could play to the Helen Archer domestic abuse story. Kate's South African partner Lucas made only a brief visit to Ambridge, and their children have yet to appear, mentioned only when they speak to their mother on Skype. Ian, the only remaining Irish character, since the convenient death of Siobhán Hathaway, has also made only rare appearances of late, but at time of going to press, some listeners still hope that his supportive friendship with Helen will be rekindled. As the chapter by William Barras in this volume indicates, Pat Archer has long since forgotten that she is Welsh, whilst on the contrary Jazzer's Scottishness reaches epic proportions. Marginalization or comic relief thus seem to be the main roles ascribed to characters who are not white and ethnically English. (For a discussion of the intersections of race, ethnicity and class in *The Archers* see Thomas 2002: 51.)

To what extent then does this sense of community, however flawed, extend beyond the programme to the listeners? And how have the fan cultures around the programme evolved in the past twenty-five years? From 1990 to 2013 the BBC played an important role in organizing the fan cultures round the programme though the official BBC fan club, the Archers Addicts. At that time, online discussions of the programme were in their infancy, but the fan club brought listeners together 'in real life'. In January 1997 I participated in an Archers Addicts weekend organized and hosted by Hedli Niklaus (who plays Kathy Perks) with – believe it or not – the assistance of Eddie Grundy (Trevor Harrison). The weekend included a quiz, a coach trip round 'Borsetshire' with lunch at 'The Bull', the performance 'From Roots to Radio by Members of the Cast and Production Team', and opportunities to meet and socialize with cast members, over drinks and meals. The fans I met in this context responded positively to these BBC initiatives – meeting up at fan club events, collecting memorabilia and autographs, and buying the merchandise marketed through the Archers Addicts fan club – all behaviours conventionally associated with fandom.

My observations at the fan club weekend and in focus groups and subsequent phone interviews led me to conclude that the version of *Archers* fandom on display here was mostly a benign affair. In my analysis of one of the groups I wrote: 'Although there is quite a lot of criticism of the programmes – about the absence of romance, the unrealistic nature of some storylines or the behaviour of some characters – fundamental loyalty is always reasserted, particularly in the face of criticism from the press' (Thomas 2002: 119). This loyalty was not just to the programme, or even the actors, but extended to include the scriptwriters and producers who were all part of a happy *Archers* family. At this time, editor Vanessa Whitburn was already quite a controversial figure, accused by one of her predecessors, William Smethurst, of 'rampant radical feminism' (Smethurst 1996: 243). There are hints of disquiet about 'Vanessa' in my notes on the Archers Addicts' discussion of the lack of romance in Ambridge at that time, but it is not long before someone intervenes in her defence:

PAM: As you say there isn't any – but then I wouldn't think Vanessa was – is a romantic sort of ...

VIV: She doesn't come across ...

ALL: No ...

PAM: Her heart – she comes across to me as quite a hard sort of ...

VIV: But we have had some nice storylines though while she's been editor.

Other, more reflexive modes of fandom were also present in this conversation, and in the other groups and interviews I did at the time I found more critical and ironic takes on the programme. Nonetheless, the dominant feature emerging from this early ethnography of *Archers* listeners is a humorous, well-disposed approach to the programme, and a belief in its quality as a rather superior soap opera, with even the more ironic fans expressing their admiration for the actors and the script, and their emotional involvement:

BEN: And I have – I have cried.

MARY: Yes. [*Laughter*] We've both –

BEN: At Shula's – at Shula's famous speech about having, you know, paid the video bill – having put – you know, the speech she did a couple of months after Mark died, when she talked about having tidied it all up and, and then there was nothing left and it was beautifully written, I think, as a kind of – and I think she's actually a very good actor. One of the best and it was actually brilliantly done and we were just ... [*Laughs*]

MARY: It was very powerful, wasn't it, the way they –

BEN: Utterly believable, and there've been a few times like that, haven't there?

The investment in the quality of *The Archers* as drama here is an important and continuing trope in the cultural significance of the programme for its mostly middle-class listeners and producers, and this was a continuing theme in my 2008 study of online fan cultures around *The Archers*. In this second phase of research I focused particularly on the *Discuss The Archers* messageboard hosted by the BBC and known as *Mustardland* because of the dominant colour of the Archers website at that time. In *Mustardland* I found a playful, but also more critical approach to the programme and to the BBC as a whole, with frequent complaints about the standard of acting and/or scripts:

– OK, I see what the SWs were trying to do, but the poor actors were given a real handful of left-overs to cope with. (Post 13, 11 August 2008, DracoM1)

– Oh, Draco, do lighten up a bit and let us have a good wallow for once. (Post 15, 11 August 2008, jennet_device)

As this extract shows, the posters adopt screen names and personae which lend a dramatic quality to their exchanges. I have argued elsewhere that the messageboards at this time were providing a 'double-dose soap' for those participating, with the online exchanges giving as much pleasure as the programme to some (Thomas 2009).

At times the critical strand in the posts leads to conflict with the pro-gramme-makers, represented by Keri Davies who then hosted the BBC Messageboards:

This – and similar comments in this thread and elsewhere – is exactly the sort of rubbish passing for criticism that I have been talking about. It demeans the writer and this messageboard and I would like it to stop, please. Please base your comments on what actually happens in the programme. (Post 31, 12 February 2008, Keri Davies)

This attempt to control the posters is followed by even more critical discussion of attempts by the BBC to censor the board. It is, however, exceptional, with Keri Davies, or Mr Keri as he was known on the board, mostly joining in with the playful and slightly ironic mode of the discussions. Already at this stage, however, Vanessa Whitburn had grave doubts about the BBC funding this highly critical space, where posters increasingly questioned the authority of the BBC and the programme-makers, and where arguably a struggle for meaning and even ownership was taking place (Thomas 2014). The critical tendency reached its apogee in January 2011, when in the sixtieth anniversary episode Nigel Pargetter fell to his death from the roof of Lower Loxley. In Ambridge the utopian community rallied round, with Hayley looking after the bereaved children, Jill Archer bringing casseroles and making lemon drizzle cake, and Shula bringing advice based on her own widowhood, while Caroline, the owner of Grey Gables, 'lent' her manager, Roy to the newly widowed Elizabeth Pargetter. And we know how well that turned out.

In contrast, on the messageboard all was rage and dissent, with one regular poster proposing an open letter to Vanessa Whitburn. The discourses I have identified as key thematics of the cultural space that is *The Archers* were replayed, with many of the protests representing Nigel's death as an attack on quality drama, the everydayness of *The Archers* and even Englishness and the rural:

> When other soaps descended to sensationalist, over-hysterical posturing, TA used to be a small haven, a semblance of a world which seemed quintessentially English. What I mourn is the fact that that 'other world' has been cruelly smashed with a kind of arbitrary lazy abandon which shows utter disrespect for the listeners and the cast! (Post 60, 5 January 2011, 'Open Letter to Vanessa Whitburn' thread)

Despite this very vocal disenchantment among *Archers* fans, the programme achieved record numbers of listeners – just over five million – a few months later, in May 2011. It is nonetheless perhaps not surprising that two years after this débâcle the BBC closed down the messageboards for good. The discussions, of course, just migrated elsewhere.

If my research indicates both the continuing prevalence of the oppositions in the *Archers'* cultural spaces (with which I opened this chapter), as well as an evolving relationship with the programme-makers, which has moved from a mostly benign disposition in the late 1990s to playful, parodic and highly critical ten years later, what then of the present day? Despite Sean O'Connor's stated commitment to the rural roots of the programme, recent storylines have consisted of a series of threats to the heritage space of Ambridge on a scale hitherto unknown. In May 2014 the pastoral setting I have described was threatened by a new major road – Route B – which would divide the village and Brookfield farm in two. David and Ruth Archer's reaction to this, as they planned to sell the farm and move north, added an even more serious threat to Ambridge as we have known it – the notion that there would be no more Archers at Brookfield. It was clear to all but the newest listeners that this simply could not happen. For the fictional world of *The Archers* to survive, Ruth and David had to maintain the heritage of Dan and Doris and Jill and Phil. Having stretched the suspension of disbelief to breaking point, the threat was partially removed in the spring of 2015 by David's change of heart – on contemplating his childhood toy farm. Almost immediately the pastoral dream became a nightmare as the River Am burst its banks and flood waters submerged the village. Here, however, as we have seen, the utopian community rose to the occasion, with heroic and not so heroic deeds, and offers of help and temporary accommodation saving the day. Then in June 2016, the hardly surprising news that the road would not be going through Ambridge after all ensured the perhaps somewhat anti-climactic salvation of the heritage space of Ambridge.

The whole Route B saga had in fact been eclipsed by the very *noir* turn the programme has taken in its in-depth exploration of emotional control and abuse through the Rob and Helen Titchener story. The pretty picture conjured by the name of their home – Blossom Hill Cottage – has been replaced by a more Hitchcockian resonance – as the cottage increasingly became Helen's prison, where she was not allowed to receive phone calls, friends or family, or even drink tea without sugar, until we finally saw her transferred to an actual prison after stabbing Rob in defence of herself and her son Henry in April 2016. In tackling this far from saccharine story the tensions between drama and the more comforting, everyday aspects of the programme have reached new heights, with listeners on Twitter begging for the story to be resolved, and for Rob's abuse of Helen to be revealed and punishment bestowed. Some have actually stopped listening, and have received encouragement on Twitter from Keri Davies, as one of the script-writers, to hang on in there: 'Listen to tonight's (Tue) on iPlayer. Very gentle stuff, I promise. Rob and Helen-free.' However, by February 2016 the story had pulled in an extra 100,000 listeners, even if the May RAJAR (Radio Joint Audience Research) figures suggest that this increase was not maintained, at least in terms of live broadcast listeners (Foster 2016). By June fans had raised over £130,000 in donations to the national domestic violence charity Refuge, demonstrating the power not only of this compelling narrative, but also of the online 'communities' around *The Archers*. On Twitter and Facebook, the online conversations often seem to be providing light relief from this intense and emotionally draining story, to say nothing of clarification from Keri Davies about what is actually going on. Online listeners commiserate and offer each other virtual gin and Valium, and enjoy parodies such as 'The Plarchers – contemporary drama in a plastic setting'. Rob in plastic is, it seems, a bit easier to cope with. At the same time serious discussions of the issues have taken place in the online fan spaces, and the donations to Refuge (see the chapter by Helen M. Burrows in this volume) clearly suggest that the programme is succeeding in the important task of raising awareness of domestic abuse and the impact of gender inequality on relationships.

The challenge for the future development of the programme, the new editor and indeed the listeners is how the balance between the elements I have discussed in this chapter will play out through the *dénouement* of the Helen and Rob story and beyond. Many listeners have found this drama so compelling that during the lighter moments of the programme they find themselves mentally, if not actually, switching off. This tendency has been compounded by the introduction of the Fairbrothers, who many consider to be irritating 'posh young things' playing at farming. Even Pip Archer (played by a new actor) and her brother Josh at times seem to fall into this category. Listeners may complain that the Rob and Helen story is too upsetting, and deploy their imaginations plotting Rob's demise, but enthusiasm for discourses on the marketing of pastured eggs and new ways of managing cattle has a tendency to wane. Nonetheless, the combination of faithful, long-term listeners who do hang on in there whatever happens, or doesn't happen, and online conversations providing an added dimension of pleasure and engagement for many seems likely to ensure the enduring success of *The Archers* in the twenty-first century. In the online spaces listeners engage creatively with the programme and some of its writers and actors, generating new meanings, and demonstrating that *The Archers* belongs to its listeners now more than ever in its history.

References

Colls, Robert, and Philip Dodd (eds) ([1986] 2014). *Englishness: Politics and Culture, 1880–1920.* London: Bloomsbury.

Dubber, Andrew (2013). *Radio in the Digital Age.* Cambridge: Polity Press.

Foster, P. (2016). '*Archers* Audience Drops Despite Domestic Abuse Drama' *The Telegraph* 19 May 2016 <http://www.telegraph.co.uk/news/2016/05/18/archers-audience-drops-despite-domestic-abuse-drama/> accessed 13 June 2016.

Geraghty, Christine (1991). *Women and Soap Opera: A Study of Prime-Time Soaps.* Cambridge: Polity Press.

Higson, Andrew (1993). 'Representing the National Past: Nostalgia and Pastiche in the Heritage Film'. In L. Friedman (ed.), *British Cinema and Thatcherism: Fires Were Started.* London: UCL Press.

O'Connor, Sean (2016). 'The 65th Anniversary Episode' <http://www.bbc.co.uk/blogs/thearchers/entries/794ad377-abc1-442c-9d81-b59d17644425> accessed 2 February 2016.

Smethurst, William (1996). *The Archers: The True Story.* London: Michael O'Mara Books.

Thomas, Lyn (2002). *Fans, Feminisms and Quality Media.* London: Routledge.

Thomas, Lyn (2009). '*The Archers*: An Everyday Story of Old and New Media', *The Radio Journal* 7.1: 49–66.

Thomas, Lyn (2014). 'Making "Quality", Class and Gender: Audiences and Producers of *The Archers* Negotiate Meaning Online'. In Helen Thornham and Simon Popple (eds), *Content Cultures: Transformations of User Generated Content in Public Service Broadcasting.* London: I. B. Tauris.

Review by Rob Titchener, Blossom Hill Cottage, Ambridge, Borsetshire

This Lyn Thomas person just does not understand anything about country life. If she did she would know that I am the only real country person in this village, and that without me the whole place would fall apart or be invaded by people from Birmingham or Bulgaria. I am one of a dying breed – and thanks to my crazy wife I nearly did die – but I am coming back and with my boys I am going to sort this place out. That Howkins chap has got this all wrong too; there is far too much emphasis on personal relationships in this place. They've all gone soft, namby pamby, chatting to each other and eating cake all day long. The place has been taken over by women and what it needs is real men keeping an eye on things and playing cricket on the green. It's not about nostalgia – we don't need Fallon's cracked cups and floral table cloths. And we definitely don't need Adam and Ian and their ilk and their sham marriage. What this place needs is clean lines and clean living. And the same goes for all those pathetic people who've got nothing better to do than tweet on a Sunday morning. If I had my way … And how dare they impersonate my stoma bag? Anyway, this kind of writing is what you can expect from a person who worked at a Polytechnic! And what did cultural studies ever do for us? I could go on but I am getting too excited and Mum says it's not good for me …

WILLIAM BARRAS

Rural Voices: What Can Borsetshire Tell Us About Accent Change?

The range of voices in The Archers *is part of its appeal as an evocation of life in an English village. This chapter will discuss the links between accent variation and the social hierarchy of characters in Ambridge, with a focus on the r sound, which is often associated in England with a rural status. By comparing Ambridge's approximate location with real-world dialect data, I will explore the significance of the Borsetshire accents typified by the Grundy, Tucker and Carter families. Other characters with less localized accents will also be discussed in the light of recent sociophonetic research. While it has traditionally been assumed that accent remains essentially constant through adult life, it is now becoming clear that adults can change aspects of their accents over time. Shula's Received Pronunciation (RP) vowels have changed subtly between 1975 and 2015 in ways which mirror changes in the wider speech community and have even been documented previously in analyses of the Queen's accent. I will discuss further intriguing cases of phonological change across the lifespan, notably the rapid shift of Pip Archer's vowel system in the space of a few months' agricultural placement in Yorkshire.*

Borsetshire's Place in English Dialectology

John Finnemore refers to 'the women with an accent' in his parody of *The Archers*, and the Grundy and Carter families do indeed have a notably rural accent when compared to other Ambridge residents. While this rural status can be signalled by vocabulary choices, non-standard grammar and certain vowel pronunciations, it is the r sound which does much of the connotative work. More precisely, it is not the phonetic sound which varies – Clarrie's r is very similar to Shula's, Jim's or Jill's – rather it is the distribution of the /r/ phoneme which is different. Characters such as Eddie,

Emma, Susan or Fallon pronounce postvocalic /r/, so there is an audible r sound in words such as farm or store: this is labelled *rhotic speech*. Other characters, including most members of the extended Archers family itself, do not have postvocalic /r/ and typically have a long vowel instead: this is *non-rhoticity*. It is interesting that a single consonant can be such a key signifier of social status in England. Actors sometimes use a strongly rhotic stereotypical 'Mummerset' accent to represent a generic rural English speech style. This rhoticity can be associated with a range of assumptions about speakers, from fairly positive notions of authenticity or the preserving of tradition, to more patronizing assumptions about a lack of education or even a lack of intelligence. Outside England, these assumptions are often reversed: some non-rhotic speech in the United States, for instance, is associated with a lack of education, and over the last few decades, rhoticity has been more-or-less consciously reintroduced into New York City speech as residents aim for a prestigious speech style in which /r/ is pronounced in postvocalic contexts.

Until very recently, the only large scale dialect survey in England was the Survey of English Dialects (SED), most of which was conducted in the 1950s. The fieldworkers often looked for the oldest inhabitant of a particular village they could find, and ideally someone who had always lived in that place. Chambers and Trudgill (1998) refer to these people as NORMs (non-mobile older rural males): modern equivalents in today's Ambridge would be people like Joe Grundy or Bert Fry. The participants would be asked a series of questions, often on rural topics associated with agriculture and the natural world, and the fieldworker would transcribe their answers phonetically. In some cases, short recordings were also made. Dialect maps generated from the survey are still used as a reference point for the geographical distribution of particular accent and dialect features, albeit with the understanding that more recent generations of speaker may have accents which have changed. Ambridge's location is slightly unclear, but we know it is fairly close to Birmingham, and several sources suggest that the real-world equivalent of Borsetshire would straddle Worcestershire and Warwickshire.

With this in mind, it is perhaps surprising to find rhoticity so strongly present in today's Ambridge. While maps based on the SED suggest that large parts of the south-west of England were rhotic, the isogloss, or dialect border, between non-rhotic and rhotic speech in the 1950s was very close to Ambridge. We know that the rhotic area has shrunk since the SED, with the isogloss moving further south and west, so in the real world we would not expect to find many rhotic speakers in Worcestershire or Warwickshire today, and certainly not younger ones. Indeed, a current research project being conducted at the University of Cambridge (Leeman and Britain 2016) uses a smartphone app in order to update the coverage of the SED. Early results from this new survey suggest that the r in arm is pronounced by very few people, even in the far south-west of England. Given this state of affairs, perhaps the speech of Emma, Fallon and the rest is not really intended to be representative of real-world trends in accents of English, but is rather a useful signifier of rural status for the BBC Radio 4 audience. The programme's strap-line is 'contemporary drama in a rural setting' so perhaps /r/ is just added to the mix along with talk of herbal leys and the idea of a single wicket competition on the village green as a gentle reminder that Ambridge is rural and pastoral rather than metropolitan and urban.

Hyper-rhoticity: A Last Gasp of Traditional Borsetshire Speech?

An additional phenomenon in the speech of the characters 'with an accent' in Ambridge is the pronunciation of r at the ends of words which have no <r> in the spelling: recently after a particularly tense phone conversation about the state of the shepherd's hut, Eddie said: 'Bye Lyndar'. The unstressed vowel at the end of words such as Lynda or Emma is called a schwa, and several Ambridge characters have a tendency to rhoticize this, so that Emma is pronounced 'Emmar' [ɛmə]. This Hyper-rhoticity pronunciation has been noted as a potential reaction against the gradual loss of rhoticity: if people around you are no longer pronouncing /r/s in all the places that you do, you might end up pronouncing as many /r/s as you possibly can, including in some words where there was no /r/ historically. Britain (2009) refers to hyper-rhoticity as a 'last gasp' of traditional English rhoticity. Even though Ambridge will be spared the intrusion of Route B, the encroachment of non-local accents might spell the end of traditional Borsetshire speech, something that may already be underway if George Grundy's accent is representative of young Ambridge residents.

Tracking Accent Change Over an Individual Speaker's Lifetime

Of course, *The Archers* is a work of fiction, and although up to this point I have been suspending my disbelief and discussing the characters as though they were real people in a real location (albeit one which is somewhat tricky to pinpoint on a map), the fact that the programme is, in effect, an archive of recordings stretching back sixty-five years, provides another avenue for linguistic research. It has traditionally been assumed that accent remains essentially constant through adult life. While young children are able to acquire new languages easily, or to change their spoken accent should they move to a different region, it seems to be much harder to do this post-adolescence. Language is always changing, and we know that as each generation of children learns to speak, there can be a gradual shift in speech sounds. The cumulative effects can be large: we know that between the fourteenth and seventeenth centuries there was a group of changes, now labelled the Great Vowel Shift, which led, for instance, to the vowel in words such as town shifting from an 'oo' sound [uː] to the 'ow' diphthong [au] which most people in England use today (though there are still indications of this earlier pronunciation in the north east of England and Scotland, where town might be toon).

However, recent research has begun to show that adults can change their phonological output over their own lifetimes. The difficulty in proving this is finding recordings of speech to work with: they need to be of the same individual person over a period of years. Ideally they would be reasonably high quality to enable quite small changes to be detected; they should also be broadly equivalent in style of speaking. A previous research project conducted by Harrington et al. (2009) used recordings of the Queen and showed that while she still speaks in a Received Pronunciation accent, some individual vowel sounds have indeed changed subtly.

I carried out a small pilot study using recordings of Judy Bennett playing Shula in 1975 and in 2015. There are some obvious differences associated with the age of the speaker: in 1975, Judy Bennett's voice occupied a slightly higher pitch range than in 2015, but differences such as that are entirely predictable based on the ways in which people's voices change with age. What is more significant is that some individual vowel sounds have altered slightly. One way in which phonologists categorize vowels is by the position of the tongue in the mouth: in "see" the tongue is high in the mouth and quite far forward in the oral cavity; in "half" the tongue is lower in the mouth and is further back in the oral cavity. These differences can be deduced from careful listening and this auditory method is how most traditional dialectology was conducted. It is also possible to measure the resonant frequencies associated with different vowels and to visualize high, low, front or back vowels by plotting these measurements on a special set of axes. This approach is particularly useful when the changes are subtle.

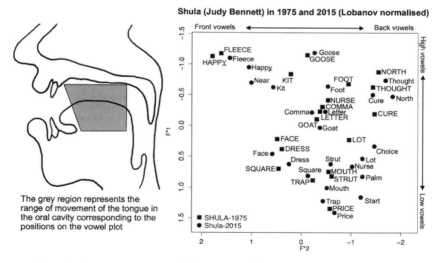

Figure 1: A comparative vowel plot generated from recordings of Judy Bennett playing Shula Archer/Shula Hebden Lloyd in 1975 and 2015. Plot generated using the NORM online suite (Thomas and Kendall 2007).

Figure 1 indicates that Shula's Received Pronunciation vowels have indeed changed subtly between 1975 and 2015. Although there are lots of vowels represented on the chart (each one identified by a key word, such as FLEECE or GOOSE) it is the TRAP vowel which is particularly interesting. Shula's 1975 pronunciation of the vowel in trap is similar to her 2015 square vowel: this is a change that Harrington et al. (2009) have noticed in recordings of the Queen, and it mirrors a change in the wider speech community. One of the reasons that the 1975 recording of Shula sounds quite old fashioned (in addition to her references to a potential boyfriend listening to jazz on his hi-fi) is the fact that when she says words such as 'dad' or 'thanks' they sound quite similar to 'dead' or 'thenks'. In contrast, by 2015 Shula's vowel in 'Dan' is lower, and indeed is very similar to the vowel that Dan himself (a younger RP speaker) has. A change like this is unlikely to be a conscious modification of speech: the phonetic shift is relatively small and it is not really something that is overtly commented on, unlike the more significant differences between northern English and southern English accents. PC Harrison Burns, for instance, has a lip-rounded [ʊ] vowel in love, while many of the Ambridge residents have an unrounded [ʌ] vowel in that word. Nonetheless, it is interesting that we can trace such changes in the speech of an individual over a period of years, and The Archers provides an excellent source of voice recordings that can be used for this purpose.

Some care must be taken when discussing The Archers data, of course. The voices we hear are those of actors reading a script, and there may be directorial influences on the characters' accents. One particularly striking case in point is that of Pat Archer, played by Patricia Gallimore from the early 1970s to the present day. Archive episodes from 1974 feature an almost unrecognizable Pat, with a strong Welsh accent, while today Pat is essentially a near-RP speaker. This sort of wholesale shift in accent is certainly possible in real life: Pat has lived in Ambridge for the last forty years and it may well be that she has naturally accommodated her speech style to match the rest of the Archer family. Such an all-encompassing change is rather different from the pattern in Shula's speech where she remained a speaker of RP, but has moved certain individual vowel sounds in the direction of younger speakers.

Recently there have been even more intriguing cases of accent change. Pip Archer had a fairly marked West Midlands accent as a teenager. Given that her mother is from Northumberland and her father is one of the RP-speaking Archers, this suggests that peer pressure and the sociocultural pull of Birmingham as the nearest big city must have been very influential on teenaged Pip. However, several months on agricultural placement in Yorkshire (and a casting change for the character) have resulted in Pip sounding somewhat different. Her vowels are now more oriented towards a general south-eastern English (popularly labelled Estuary English) and she has also developed a marked tendency to vocalize the consonant /l/ so that milk sounds like 'miwk'. A brief sojourn in Yorkshire is unlikely to have resulted in these particular accent changes. While of course there can be all sorts of reasons for recasting characters, and while I have shown that individual speakers can indeed change their accents over time, very sudden changes in accent may be somewhat jarring for the audience.

Future Research

The analysis of Shula's vowel changes above only scratches the surface of what is possible. As *The Archers* is broadcast six evenings each week, it will be possible to conduct much more fine-grained analysis of change over time. If we know that an individual has changed a particular vowel pronunciation by looking at two snapshots of data, forty years apart, then the next step would be to examine a whole series of intermediate recordings in order to see whether this was a gradual movement or a sudden jump, and whether any other accent features changed over the same time period. Within the world of Ambridge, it will be interesting to see if the younger Grundys grow up maintaining the rhoticity of their parents' generation or whether Ambridge will become entirely non-rhotic.

References

Britain, David (2009). 'One Foot in the Grave? Dialect Death, Dialect Contact, and Dialect Birth in England', *International Journal of the Sociology of Language* 196/197: 121–55

Chambers, J. K., and Peter Trudgill (1998). *Dialectology*. Cambridge: Cambridge University Press.

Harrington, Jonathan, Sallyanne Palethorpe and Catherine Watson (2009). 'Monophthongal Vowel Changes in Received Pronunciation: An Acoustic Analysis of the Queen's Christmas Broadcasts', *Journal of the International Phonetic Association* 30.1/2: 63–78.

Finnemore, John (2012). *John Finnemore's Souvenir Programme*, Series 2, Episode 2. BBC Radio 4.

Leeman, Adrian, and David Britain (2016). 'Cambridge App Maps Decline in Regional Diversity of English Dialects' <https://www.cam.ac.uk/research/news/cambridge-app-maps-decline-in-regional-diversity-of-english-dialects> accessed 15 June 2016.

Thomas, Erik R., and Tyler Kendall (2007). 'NORM: The Vowel Normalization and Plotting Suite' <http://ncslaap.lib.ncsu.edu/tools/norm/> accessed 15 June 2016.

Review by Shula Hebden Lloyd, The Stables, Ambridge, Borsetshire

Well, I'm in two minds about what I've just read. Of course, I think it's lovely that our traditional Borsetshire way of speaking is still alive and well. It's all part of what makes Ambridge such a special place and it's always so nice to chat to Clarrie after church on Sundays. And it's wonderful that the next generation are keeping this up: Fallon and Emma are wonderful examples of young Borsetshire businesswomen who are proud of their local accent. Of course, I'm not sure it'd be appropriate for Daniel – sorry, Dan – to speak with quite such a ... noticeable accent. He's been to Sandhurst, you know, and his soldiers are bound to

expect a slightly more refined style of speaking from their com-
manding officer. As for the section on my accent, I'm somewhat
perplexed. I suppose it's good to learn that I am moving with the
times, although I'm not sure I've noticed my accent changing.
I think so long as any changes are not too drastic then it's fine;
I'm really not sure I'd want to end up speaking like the Button
girls, however; they never shut-up. And Sabrina Thwaite does
go on endlessly. I must show this to Jim, although to be honest I
don't think he really approves of any changes in language: Latin
is more his style. Mind you, perhaps Jazzer's influence will rub
off on him eventually.

NEIL MANSFIELD AND LAUREN MORGAN

Tony Archer the Farmer: The Toll of Life as an Agricultural Worker and Changing Technology in Modern Farming

Life has been physically tough for Tony Archer. Quite apart from the family stresses coming to their crescendo in 2016, he has worked hard on the farm for his entire life. The farming world has changed substantially since he was born in 1951, but he has made efforts to work close to nature, and has remained a hands-on farmer, even as he transitions into retirement. The rigours of farming have taken their toll with his long-standing back pain. He has lost a son to a farming accident caused by a tractor roll-over, and almost lost his own life in an incident involving Otto the bull. This chapter will use Tony's experience in farming to illustrate the contemporary life of a farmer focusing on the workload and physical stresses of the work. It will also look towards the future of farming, taking examples from Ambridge of those areas where technology has potential to make a difference to farming life.

Tony Archer's Tractor

Tony Archer has complained of trouble with his back for years. Pat has even threatened to send him to the chiropractor, although Tony resisted such 'hocus pocus' (2008). The problem of back pain in agriculture is well known and unsurprising considering the manual handling, postural stresses, long working hours and exposure to vibration and shocks whilst driving agricultural machines. Tractor design has moved on over the decades such that today we have a plethora of manufacturers producing machines ranging from sixteen-horsepower-compact machines, through to large complex models with over thirty times the power and a price tag of close to £250,000. Historically the design comprised two large driven wheels at the rear and two small wheels at the front. Since the 1990s four-wheel drive and improved suspension has become commonplace on modern farms allowing for more usable power and versatility. Originally tractors simply towed an implement. It is now standard for tractors to have a three-point hitch and power lines at the rear enabling precise control of the towed tooling (for example, ploughs, spreaders and sprayers or trailers). Similarly the standard 'Power Take Off' (PTO) allows for rotary power to be transmitted into the towed implement directly from the gearbox (see Figure 2).

Figure 2: A modern 110 HP tractor (left) and a farmer attaching an implement to the PTO (right).

A wide variety of tractors are referred to in *The Archers*. Several vintage machines have been restored over the years, and even used in competitive ploughing competitions (e.g. Bert Fry vs. Jimmy Prentice), or been the subject of controversy (e.g. Ed and Jazzer buying, restoring and selling on a machine at significant profit from a widowed customer in 2013). At the other end of the scale, contractors such as Adam Macy and Home Farm use complex machines, potentially with Global Positioning System (GPS) assistance as demonstrated at Open Farm Sunday in June 2016. Ed Grundy provides services using an unknown machine; details are scarce apart from the fact that it is green, had 3,000 hours on the clock when it was purchased, and has needed some regular servicing.

Whilst tractors may now include technologies that were unthinkable in the 1940s, the tasks that are completed are fundamentally similar, in terms of cultivation and harvest of crops. Images of 'Land Girls' from the Second World War often show them driving tractors with towed implements and showing a twisted posture. Seventy years on, this posture is still commonly adopted by agricultural workers for extended periods of the working day (see Figure 3). A twisted posture has been shown to be poor not only from

Figure 3: The 'Land Girl' posture is still used in modern tractors where controls are still located behind the driver.

a health perspective but also for comfort, workload and task performance (e.g. Newell and Mansfield 2008). At some times of the year working hours in this poor position can be extremely long. For example, hedgerows must not be cut between 1 March and 31 July in order for the farm to qualify for the EU Single Farm Payment, meaning that the job must be completed in a finite period at specific times of year. This time restriction is to minimize adverse impact of wildlife, especially nesting birds. The work requires the use of a rear-mounted cutter on a hydraulic boom which is manoeuvred from the cab and carefully positioned to ensure a clean and sufficient cut but keeping the tractor safe and avoiding contact with trees and other obstacles. A similar process is used for ditches and culverts, such as those secretly cleared by Ed Grundy in spring 2015, following the Ambridge flood. The process of hedge and ditch work means that the driver's attention is constantly split between facing forwards to drive safely, and facing rearwards to monitor the cutter/bucket. Thus the driver spends the entire task repeatedly twisting whilst driving and being exposed to whole-body vibration and shock.

Farm Health and Safety

The EU Physical Agents (Vibration) Directive (2002) aims to protect all workers from the hazards of vibration of the hands and the whole-body, such as those experienced in tractors. It should be noted that the UK Regulations derived from this Directive have been very successful in reducing the vibration exposure, and therefore the health risks, in many industries and the fact that changes to working patterns have been necessary is an indicator of successful risk reduction interventions. Whole-body vibration in tractors is usually greater than the 'Exposure Action Value' meaning that action must be taken by the employer to minimize risks. It can sometimes exceed the 'Exposure Limit Value' if working hours are long such as during harvest periods; the Exposure Limit Value is a legal limit which must not be exceeded. One effective way of reducing the vibration is to install a high-quality suspension seat which isolates the driver from vibration and shock; however these can be costly and need to be specified, installed and set-up correctly for each driver (Mansfield 2005). Tony would likely have been exposed to vibration that exceeded the Exposure Action Value on most days that he worked with his machinery, and would have frequently been exposed above the Limit Value. *The Archers* indicates that on those days when he is not operating a tractor, he was often carrying out other physically demanding tasks. Even despite having back pain, he still continued to work, feeling like he had no choice but to put up with his ailments. This is a common phenomenon across all industries characterized by the self-employed, where personal health is compromised in order to maintain the success of the business.

Annually, 4–5 per cent of workers in agriculture, forestry and fishing experience a reportable injury. The benchmark across all occupations is 2 per cent. Of these injuries about 40 per cent are either a slip/trip or animal-related injury. Musculoskeletal disorders such as back and neck pain formed the majority of self-reported illness in the agriculture, forestry and fishing sector in 2014/2015 (HSE 2015). The prevalence of musculoskeletal disorders for agriculture is approximately double that of 'all occupations'. Over the past decade there has been no clear improvement in these statistics. In the five years from 2010/11 to 2014/15 there were 160 fatal injuries in the sector, approximately two to three per month (see Figure 4); the annual rate of 9.1 per 100,000 workers (14/15) is higher than any other sector. For comparison, in 'construction' and 'all industries' the rates are 1.6 and 0.5 per 100,000 respectively. Of the fatalities in agriculture there were twenty-three cases where the fatality was caused by injury caused by an animal. In November 2014 Tony Archer was seriously injured by Otto the bull, and came close to being another victim. In this case a routine task of moving cattle suddenly escalated due to small unpredictable events that scared the animal. After some time in hospital Tony recovered to return to the farm. Otto did not survive. John Archer, Tony's son, was killed in a tractor accident in February 1998; a case of a rollover of an old tractor. Rollover protection systems and seatbelts have been standard tractor equipment for many decades, although remain optional for smaller estate maintenance vehicles and mowers. The UK Health and Safety Executive recommend rollover protection even for the smallest vehicles (Scarlett et al. 2006).

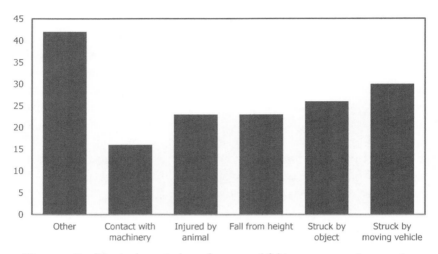

Figure 4: Fatalities in the agriculture, forestry and fishing sector 2010/11–2014/15
(data from the HSE).

In a survey of expert opinion on back pain in agriculture (Morgan and Mansfield 2014) experts in the fields of human response to vibration, ergonomics/posture and farming (operators) were asked their opinion of how and why back pain occurred in agriculture. When asked how long it was acceptable to work operating a tractor, the farmers gave the longest times, followed by the vibration experts. The posture experts were most conservative with exposure times, recommending working times of three or less hours, on average, even in the most ideal postures. Under conditions of 'high twist' the farmers considered exposure times of three to four hours to be acceptable, likely based on their own operation experience. However, the vibration and posture experts were far more conservative and recommended exposure times of less than an hour. Each group was asked its opinion on where back pain would occur when exposed to whole-body vibration, postural stress (twisting) or a combination. Whilst all groups considered pain in the lower back to be the most prevalent for vibration, there were differences for the other conditions. The farmers did not report low back pain when twisted, but just neck pain. The other groups expected to see low back pain and either neck or upper back pain (see Figure 5). Farmers specifically targeted neck, right shoulder and low back for pain related to

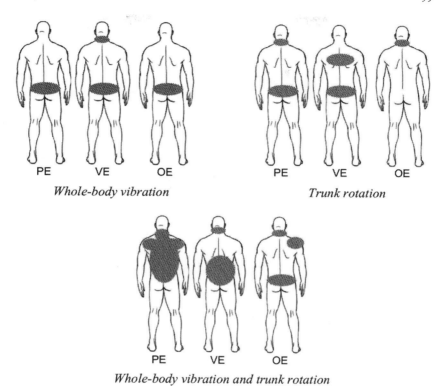

Figure 5: A survey of expert opinion on back pain in agriculture: shaded areas indicate where less than 40 per cent of experts predicted discomfort under the different exposure combinations (Posture Experts (PE), n = 35; Vibration Experts (VE), n = 13; Operator (Farming) Experts (OE), n = 22). Figure reproduced from Morgan and Mansfield (2014) with permission.

combined twisting and vibration. Tractor operators almost always twist to the right, as this is where tools tend to be operated and the secondary instrument panel(s) are located (see again Figure 3); it is therefore logical that they would expect to experience pain on that side.

Farmers were keen on swivelling seats but these were not considered as beneficial by the other groups; only about one third of posture experts would recommend them. CCTV was not considered desirable by farmers but was considered good by the posture and vibration experts (see Figure 5). These data show that the opinions of farmers do not necessarily

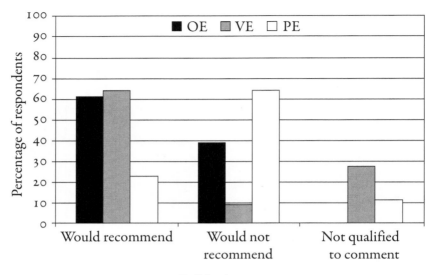

Full backrest seat

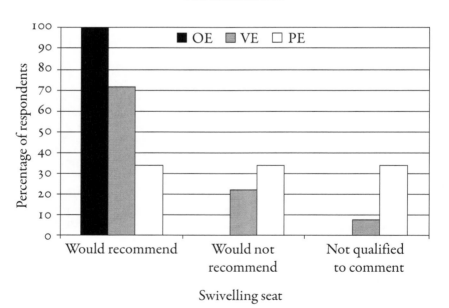

Swivelling seat

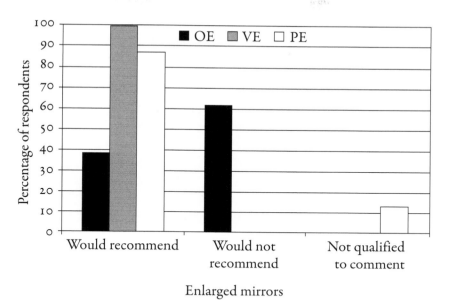

Enlarged mirrors

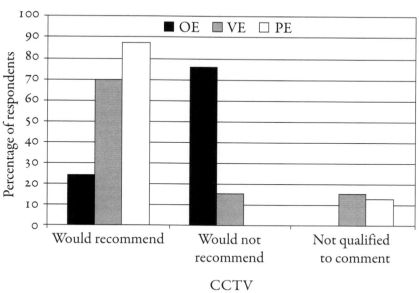

CCTV

Figure 6: Expert opinion of common recommendations for reducing risk for lower back pain from occupational exposures with trunk rotation and WBV exposure: (Operator (Farming) Experts (OE), n = 23; Vibration Experts (VE), n = 13; Posture Experts (PE), n = 9). Figure reproduced from Morgan and Mansfield (2014) with permission.

match those of technical experts. The strong opinions regarding the issues related to visibility could indicate that farmers feel that their workplace is sufficiently designed already in that aspect; however the opinion regarding the swivel seat shows that this would a very popular option in agricultural machines. Considering the differences in expert opinion, it is important that recommendations are based on empirical evidence of benefit (or otherwise) and this requires independent research. Unfortunately rural research is a low priority in comparison to opportunities afforded for city and urban issues.

Technological Developments in Agriculture

Borsetshire farmers have mixed opinions on the latest technologies. David, Ruth and Pip Archer carefully considered the potential benefit of robotic milking, but ultimately decided on a simpler approach to milk, minimizing up-front costs and technical investments. Milking machines have been standard on UK farms for over a century and slashed the time needed to milk a herd, allowing for larger herds to be feasible. These systems still require manual application of teat cups and work using a pulsed vacuum. A robotic milker works by automating gates and application of the milking unit itself. Cows can choose when they are ready to be milked and the system does not allow over-milking based on monitoring individual cows via ID tags. This can eliminate the need for farmers to be present during early morning milking, thereby radically changing the routine which has become familiar amongst the dairy farmers in Ambridge. Tony took delight in the fact the he would no longer need such early starts when Bridge Farm sold their dairy herd.

Prototype autonomous tractors have been in existence since the 2000s and are capable of performing simple tasks by using GPS navigation. Automated driving means more repeatable route keeping resulting in a smaller 'tyreprint', thus maximizing the cultivatable land, in addition to the potential of removing the operator from the machine. On the largest farms (such as many in the USA) it is possible for one operator to control a fleet of machines working together. In addition, it is already possible to map the detailed profile of land including soil composition, aspect to light, shelter and exposure, so that spraying can be controlled optimally based on a concept of 'plant by plant' rather than delivering the same chemical uniformly across an entire field, even if there are no plants growing in that area. This minimizes wastage hence minimizing potential chemical run-off. Autonomous aerial vehicles ('drones'), similar to that used with great enthusiasm by Charlie Thomas in spring 2015, also have a place in future farming. Whilst the opportunity to inspect crops with high definition cameras is obvious, it is also possible to herd animals using the technology. Some have been developed to drop 'plug' plants into inaccessible areas (e.g. forestry), but this is currently expensive and slow. The boom in the 'app' market that has affected so many industries has not missed out farming, many of the apps focus on supporting crop/pest identification for arable farming, or stock management for meat and dairy farming. Many are provided free of charge to the farming community, but their use is not yet widespread.

The Archers provides a window on many of the issues facing twenty-first-century agriculture with an understandable focus on the human issues. If the drama continues to reflect farming we will unfortunately continue to hear of accidents and injuries, but also of new technologies and developments in equipment. All new developments in agriculture still require a human operator somewhere in the system, and need expert operators on-the-ground in order to install, maintain and deal with the unpredictability of working with nature. For the foreseeable future there will remain the need for Archer, Grundy and other families to keep the UK agricultural industry in business.

References

European Parliament and the Council of the European Union (2002). Directive 2002/44/EC on the minimum health and safety requirements regarding the exposure of workers to the risks arising from physical agents (vibration), OJ L177 edn, *Official Journal of the European Communities*.

Newell, G. S., and Mansfield, N. J. (2008). 'Evaluation of Reaction Time Performance and Subjective Workload During Whole-Body Vibration Exposure While Seated in Upright and Twisted Postures With and Without Armrests', *International Journal of Industrial Ergonomics* 38: 499–508.

Health and Safety Executive (2015). *Health and Safety in Agriculture, Forestry and Fishing in Great Britain, 2014/2015* <http://www.hse.gov.uk/statistics/> accessed 27 June 2016.

Mansfield, N. J. (2005). *Human Response to Vibration*. Boca Raton, FL: CRC Press.

Morgan, L. J., and Mansfield, N. J. (2014). 'A Survey of Expert Opinion on the Effects of Occupational Exposures to Trunk Rotation and Whole-Body Vibration', *Ergonomics* 57.4: 563–74.

Review by Ed Grundy, c/o Neil and Susan Carter, Ambridge View, Ambridge, Borsetshire

I've lived on a farm all my life and I can tell you it's hard. I was there when Tony and Henry almost got killed and you have to remember that bulls have a mind of their own and although you can love them, you can't trust them. You sometimes have to act fast and take control and Tony was lucky that Johnny kept calm and did what he was told. But that's what us farmers do: we look out for each other and muck in when we see others in trouble. You never know when you're going to need help yourself, and unless you have a load of money to bankroll you, like my brother or Borsetshire Land, you can need help to stay in business. But sometimes you still can't make ends meet and you can lose your livelihood and that's really tough. I don't like talking about when I lost my herd, but when it happened I knew I needed to get up to date with the tech. It's amazing some of the stuff you see at the shows and what I've got is basic in comparison. You've got to get trained and I know if George and Keira want to carry on in the family trade they need to get qualified. You know, until I read this, I'd never really thought about how much you have to twist round when you're doing stuff like ditches and hedges; although you're not doing heavy lifting, you can really feel it at the end of the day. I'm not very impressed with the idea that you're supposed to limit hours during harvest. That's impossible! The crop in the fields is money and when it's ready we need to bring it in – what are we supposed to do, get a robot to do it or something?

ABI PATTENDEN

Seeming, Seeming: *Othello, The Archers* and Rob Titchener

This chapter will examine how the representation of Rob Titchener within The Archers *draws comparison with some of the themes in Shakespeare's* Othello, *specifically in terms of his exploitation of other characters' weaknesses. It will also look at how the importance of reputation affects Rob's relationships.*

Introduction

In *Othello*, the eponymous title character, a well-respected general, is manipulated by his ensign, Iago, after he promotes Cassio to lieutenant. Iago feels he should have received this advancement and vows revenge. Assisted – often unwittingly – by various characters within the play, Iago convinces Othello that his wife, Desdemona, has been cuckolding him with Cassio. Iago engineers some bad behaviour on Cassio's part and subsequently suggests Desdemona helps him to regain the general's favour. This conspiracy appears to Othello to be evidence of their affair. Iago's wife, Emilia, steals a handkerchief from Desdemona and gives it to her husband, not realizing why he wants it. Iago plants the handkerchief on Cassio and so gives Othello what seems to be irrefutable proof of his wife's infidelity. The play ends with the death of Desdemona and Emilia at their respective husbands' hands, before the truth is revealed and Othello, in despair, takes his own life.

Rob Titchener, like Iago, shows skills in manipulation. He escaped his deception with his life, but Helen proved to be more perceptive than Othello; she realized what Rob was doing and challenged him. Othello only finds out the truth once Desdemona is dead. Also, Rob did not attain the revenge that Iago did: Helen, unlike Othello, survived. Both sets of characters find there are implications to 'seeming', but the value of reputation in the world of *Othello* means the stakes for those who deceive are – inevitably – higher.

Iago and Rob: Perceptive Exploiters

Iago knows that Othello 'thinks men are honest that but seem to be so'. He abuses this weakness accordingly, as he does with other major characters within the play. Equally, Rob assessed many of Ambridge's residents and found characteristics he could exploit. Shula's lie about the confrontation between Rob and the hunt sab seemed unlikely for Borsetshire's saintly Shula, but she told Rob herself why she lied: out of loyalty to Helen and the hunt. Rob seemed to take this for granted, suggesting that he had already judged that her well-established sense of morality was not, in fact, her primary motivator.

Rob's actions 'seem' to have entirely different intentions. He constantly convinced Helen he was thinking of her, whilst his true motivations were self-serving. When he persuaded her to sell Ambridge Organics (ostensibly so she didn't miss out on Henry's childhood) the listener knew really he wanted her at home. At Ian and Adam's wedding, his faux-admiration of Ian's 'understanding' of Adam's infidelities was actually designed to undermine that relationship. The examples of him convincing Pat that he had Helen's best interests at heart – whilst driving a wedge between them – are too numerous to list, and were so effective that, after the stabbing, Pat told the police that he was a doting husband.

Reputation

Iago gets Cassio drunk, and he disgraces himself in this state. Again, Iago uses his judgement of others' flaws, correctly guessing that overindulgence will make Cassio 'full of quarrel .../As my young mistress' dog'. Othello witnesses Cassio's behaviour and judges accordingly: his 'rich opinion' of him is replaced by viewing him as a 'night-brawler'. Cassio is devastated by the loss of 'the immortal part of/myself' which his reputation represents and is concerned – rightly – that this inadvertent deception will be effective and now Othello will assume that his previous good conduct was fake, and that his 'drunken … indiscreet' behaviour is the reality. He says he would rather Othello 'despised' him than believe he has lied. Subsequently, Iago criticizes those who 'seem', creating a state of opposites where those who deceive can never be 'honest'. Othello's quick decision makes clear the risks of being caught 'seeming'. Reputation is both important and fragile, a dangerous combination.

Rob is always concerned with the maintenance of his reputation. He will use his manipulative skills to ensure he remains in his self-imposed place at the top of the hierarchy. For example when he, Tom and Pat discussed Tom's decision to stock non-organic meat in the Farm Shop on 21 January 2016:

> Rob: I thought it would be helpful to have the new ordering policy spelled out.
>   […]
> Pat: [*On being told the rules viz. organic had been relaxed*] Are we doing that?
> Rob: Well, we seem to be.
>   […]
> Rob: It's simply knowing where the new boundaries lie.
>   […]
> Pat: Of course you and Helen will decide, Rob.
> Rob: Ah, well, that wasn't quite clear.

Rob stays ever-reasonable. He is skilled with language, using words such as 'simply', suggesting that what he's asking for is rational. He uses qualifiers – we 'seem' to be doing things, things are not 'quite' clear – which make his message milder. What he wants is 'helpful', associating positive qualities with his perspective. He often has a light tone of voice which rarely alters, despite the tone of others – and a distinctive chuckle. He is persistent in achieving concessions but, once he has done so, he always appears magnanimous. These tactics combine to make concerns about acceding to his requests seem churlish. As well as getting what he wants, he is also bolstering his reputation as the person to be deferred to.

Many of Rob's criticisms of Helen were ostensibly around his reputation. Accusations of undermining him and hurting his pride left her unable to make decisions for herself, the consequence being that she acquiesced to a home birth she didn't want rather than 'embarrass him' in front of Ursula – who he claimed knew best.

Unforeseen Consequences

Significant instances of deception in *Othello* occur although the character is unaware of their implications. When Emilia steals Desdemona's handkerchief for Iago, she has no idea what he will do with it, only that he has asked her 'a hundred times' to do so; but Iago is then able to use it as the ultimate piece of evidence of the supposed affair between Cassio and Desdemona. Both Desdemona and Helen 'seem', and, like Emilia, their actions have unforeseen consequences.

Desdemona's initial 'seeming' is deliberate. She married Othello while deceiving her father about their true relationship. According to her father, prior to this event she has been 'a jewel', but he responds to her deception by suggesting that it sets a precedent for her future conduct:

> Look to her, Moor ...
> She has deceived her father, and may thee.

Iago has seen from Othello's treatment of Cassio that he shares society's view of 'seeming' as a constant. This straightforward attitude to morality makes Iago's revenge easy, as Desdemona's previous deceit gives him the ammunition he needs:

> She that ... could give out such a seeming
> To seal her father's eyes up close as oak-
> He thought 'twas witchcraft.

Othello knows she can 'seem' and so (despite his earlier complicity) he expects her to do so again. (Interestingly, his own deception of her father doesn't come into his consideration.)

In contrast, Helen's 'seeming' was accidental. However, it also led to a misperception of her – by Rob. On the night that Jack/Gideon was conceived, 27 August 2015, Rob told Helen about his first impressions of her:

> I remember ... you were sitting by yourself in the playground with Henry ... laughing ... I thought to myself ... What lucky so-and-so got her to give him a child? ... you're a wonderful mother ... beautiful and devoted.

By the time this conversation took place, it was clear that he had misjudged her. He took her for a happy mother to Henry, needing no one else, and assumed from this that she would want more children. Helen protests his incorrectness about 'that woman' as if she was someone else, distancing herself from the person he thought he saw. However, Rob disagrees: 'You're perfect.' It appears that Rob targeted Helen as a potential partner based on his assumptions – especially around her maternal instincts. He always made his desire for a family clear; he told Helen that Jess's unwillingness to have children was a major cause of their relationship breakdown – although the listener later heard from Jess that this was untrue. These assumptions, resulting from Helen's accidental 'seeming', led to many of the subsequent events. She tried to put obstacles to children in his path, but he pushed them aside. The astute listener may have realized that lack of marriage was her only credible defence and therefore, once she agreed to their 'quickie' wedding, she had run out of excuses. Arguably this rape, which led to the conception, happened because Rob realized that there was no prospect of Helen agreeing to have more children for the foreseeable future – having invested so much in his assumption, and unwilling to be incorrect, he removed consent from the equation.

Again, his skills at language are on display and hint at the events to come. He told Helen that he'd wanted to know who 'got her' to have a child. He highlights one of his mistaken assumptions – a relationship between Helen and Henry's father – even as he foreshadows his intention to be wrong in his others. He outlines his expectations – that a child is something a mother gives, but passively. The man 'gets her' to have the child, as Rob will when he rapes her that night.

Self-Fulfilling Prophecies

In both instances, what Desdemona and Helen 'seemed' to be, becomes reality. Desdemona, suspected of being dishonest after one instance of deception, proves herself a liar when she tells Othello that the handkerchief – which he knows she doesn't have – is 'not lost'. It was his first gift to her, so she knew it was important, but he amplifies its significance, claiming that it belonged to his mother, who believed it had magical properties. Her lie – motivated by fear of this value – appears to him to confirm her status as a 'seemer', and proves everything that Iago has alleged about her. She could not have anticipated the implications of her lie to her father, but there is a causal link in the narrative between that one-off deception and her fate. Equally, Rob's actions towards Helen – keeping her at home, criticizing her outfits and opinions, and ultimately the multiple rapes – created, and then maintained, the isolated, demure mother that she 'seemed' to him to be.

Revenge as Motivation

Iago cites his desire for revenge within the first few lines of the play, saying that he wants 'to serve my turn upon [Othello]'. We learn later that his revenge has a sexual dimension because he believes that "twixt my sheets/ [Othello] has done my office'. There is no evidence within the play of any relationship between Othello and Emilia, but it gives Iago's actions an added reciprocal motivation, as his plan leads to Othello suspecting he has been cuckolded in his turn.

I would suggest that Rob is also motivated by revenge. It is arguable that his control of Helen is revenge on her for her 'seeming'. He mistook her for something she wasn't; this must be hard to accept for someone who is expert at reading people, and so concerned with his reputation. When he finally realized that she would never accede to his control, his solution was to eliminate her. This idea is reinforced when you consider Rob's relationship with Charlie. Like most of Ambridge, Rob seems to have assumed that Charlie was straight.

His long-established homophobia amplifies the significance of this mistake, already important as his self-image includes his ability to judge others accurately. It also damages his idea of the world and his 'rightness' within it – it's easy to imagine what Rob thinks gay men are like, and he has discovered he is not always correct. On finding he was wrong, he deployed his language skills to imply Charlie's sexuality rendered him amoral, and non-sympathetic to 'conventional' family life. Rob's dislike of Charlie came not only from his aversion to gay men but also because he was taken in by Charlie's 'seeming', and his actions of revenge are his way of removing evidence of his fallibility. Rob seems to have accepted that changing Charlie is not possible, as changing Helen might have been. In both cases we see him trying to remove those who have fooled him, seeking revenge for their ability to threaten his perception of himself.

Manipulation to the Last

Once Iago's actions are revealed, Othello begs him to explain himself but, ever the manipulator, he refuses, stating that 'From this time forth I never will speak word'. Although justice – in the form of a torturous death – is promised, Othello is denied the truth. Many listeners felt sure that Helen's stabbing of Rob would lead to his ultimate comeuppance, and would indeed have welcomed it. In retrospect, this was unlikely for several reasons, not least the differing mediums concerned. It is inevitable that a play will have a finite conclusion which leads to resolution for the audience (if not the characters), while the serial nature of *The Archers* means that storylines and characters have to develop. The precedent set by *Othello* suggests that Rob will continue his deceitful path, spewing vitriol against Helen and her violent tendencies while 'seeming' to be the innocent victim. His determination to present her as a crazed aggressor seems strange for someone who needs to be seen as the strong one, but is the logical continuation of his attempts to be revenged on her for her ultimate refusal to accept his control. There is no positive resolution for either Iago or Othello in the play. Whether things end well for Helen, Rob, or neither, remains to be seen.

Reference

Shakespeare, William (2016). *Othello*. London: Bloomsbury Arden Shakespeare (2nd rev. edn).

Review by Pat Archer, Bridge Farm, Ambridge, Borsetshire

Rob seemed to be the ideal husband, didn't he? And Helen seemed so happy. That was all we ever wanted for her. I remember, when she was born, I was so pleased to have my little girl. Helen's always been so fragile. Tony was always telling me to leave well alone – well, we didn't want to risk not seeing Henry. And Rob seemed to care about her so much. He always seemed to know exactly what to say. He always had an answer and he just seemed so reasonable. We knew Helen was tired but we thought with the not eating, and the baby … I never suspected anything could be wrong. She told me so often everything was alright. Every time I saw her, every time I asked, she told me things were fine and she was happy. Rob was so reassuring, so calm, he seemed to understand everything. I should have seen through him. Kirsty did, and Tom had begun to, too. And, now, all of this. Having Jack in prison! Without me! It's so unfair, I should have been able to be with her. She needed me. And I wanted to see her so badly. Why didn't they realize that she wouldn't hurt a fly? I know Rob says she was unhinged, but surely that can't be true. Can it? I don't want to doubt her but, as Tony says, 'we know what Helen's like'. It's all so wrong.

HELEN M. BURROWS

An Everyday Story of Dysfunctional Families: Using *The Archers* in Social Work Education

Social work students need to understand the difficulties that their future service users may experience. Learning is developed through lectures, seminars and workshops, and most of all through practice placements, but a real challenge for social work educators is how to show students the constant lived reality of families who have complex difficulties. An hour's visit to a family only gives a snapshot of that point in time, and service users may be guarded in their behaviour when a professional visits. This chapter considers the educational value of the 'fly-on-the-wall' perspective of The Archers, *in catching unguarded moments. Recently the Helen and Rob Titchener storyline has accurately portrayed domestic abuse and doubtful parenting. Other examples include the impact of rural poverty, caring for a relative through progressive Alzheimer's disease, and issues of substance misuse and criminal behaviour. The chapter also considers the use of 'fan pages' in social media, as a method for in-depth discussion of students' learning, and the discussion of social work values and ethics.*

Introduction

Social workers have often been stereotyped as *Guardian*-reading Radio 4 listeners; whilst we would of course be absolutely against any stereotyping, it has to be said that many of us have been known to sit in car parks between visits to listen to the lunchtime broadcast – it was even a social work colleague who introduced me to the Archers Anarchists, whose motto is 'The Archers is real, there is no cast!'

In this chapter I will show how listening to *The Archers* can contribute to social work education, with particular reference to the story of Rob and Helen Titchener's dysfunctional relationship, and look at the role of social media fan pages in developing understanding of issues.

The Role and Structure of Social Work Education

Social work students encounter many different family and individual situations during their training, and need to understand the difficulties that their
future service users may experience. None of us have innate knowledge of
all the problems that may be met in social work practice, so what do social
work students learn and how does this learning take place? Students have
to develop the knowledge, skills and values required by the Professional
Capabilities Framework (TCSW 2012). Nine domains of learning cover
everything from professionalism, values and ethics; through to knowledge, intervention and skills. Basic capability is developed and broadened
through the qualifying course, and then throughout a professional career.
Most social workers qualify through a three year first degree or two year
Masters course; learning is developed through lectures, seminars and two
hundred days of practice placements, which are generally in two different
settings so that they can develop generic skills.

The social work placement is maybe the most important learning
opportunity for social work students (Domakin 2015); they are supervised
by a qualified practice educator and sometimes an additional on-site super-
visor, and given the opportunity to apply classroom learning to real life
practice in skill development. Working with service users and carers can
be a big 'reality shock', when students will experience unfamiliar situations
and may not know what they will find from hour to hour when out in the
community. They will learn about procedures and legislation – and to
apply these sensitively and carefully, for it is real lives that they are dealing
with. However difficult this may seem, it really is the best way of learning,
as Irvine et al. (2015: 144) suggest: 'Learning from someone "in the flesh"
had far more of a lasting impression than other forms of teaching.'

However placements do not necessarily give insight into the lived
experience of the individuals and families. Families can be wary of professionals, who can have the power to provide or refuse services, and in
some cases impose conditions on how families live, including compulsory
admissions to hospital, or the removal of children into care. Additionally,
placements are relatively short-term, so it can be difficult for people to

trust a student who they know will be 'handing them on' to someone else when their placement ends. Even with the best working relationships, an hour's visit can only ever provide a snapshot of how people are living and interacting. As professionals, we will rarely see life as it is lived all the time. This is where *The Archers* can come into its own, in allowing us to catch unguarded moments which a professional would never see (or hear).

So What Can *The Archers* Teach Social Workers About?

The Archers gives us a fly-on-the-wall insight into the daily lives of the residents of Ambridge, which – whilst it may have its strange aspects, such as a lack of BBC Radio 4 and its own micro-climate – is in itself a microcosm of English society, with all its strengths and wonderful eccentricities, and reflects the issues that can be found in the majority of communities. We obviously hear about farming issues in real time; you may remember the difficulties experienced at Brookfield during the Foot and Mouth outbreak in 2001 – and this was always one of the points of the programme in the first place. However, we have also experienced more general social issues in recent years including racism against Usha, drug and alcohol problems, armed robbery at the village shop and other criminal activities, rural poverty, homelessness, caring for a relative through progressive Alzheimer's disease, disabled children (though remarkably few adults unless you count Brian's transient epilepsy and Mike's missing eye) and changing attitudes towards gay relationships. Of course the village's social issues have always fed into the narrative in a big way – recently the *Guardian* (Clapp 2016) considered the ten best *Archers* storylines to include Jennifer's out-of-wedlock pregnancy in 1966, the criminal activities of the Horrobin family and Susan Carter's subsequent imprisonment in 1993 (we had a 'Free the Ambridge One' poster up in the office), Jack Woolley's dementia, numerous deaths where there were serious health and safety concerns (notably John Archer's and Nigel Pargetter's), and of course Helen and Rob Titchener's strained and dysfunctional relationship.

I have been listening to *The Archers* since 1964, but it was only recently, when a student I was supervising on placement wanted to learn more about domestic violence, that I talked to him about Helen and Rob, and realized how much he and other students and professionals could learn if they started to listen in. So what might he have learned? At the time, there were many listeners expressing doubts on social media as to whether Rob's treatment of Helen could be described as 'domestic violence', as it appeared that he had never struck her. As things have developed, I think that we can be clear that it can be seen now in no other way – it fits the definition given in the practice direction for family courts almost word for word:

- 'Domestic violence' includes any incident or pattern of incidents of controlling, coercive or threatening behaviour, violence or abuse [...]. This can encompass, but is not limited to, psychological, physical, sexual, financial, or emotional abuse.
- 'Controlling behaviour' means an act or pattern of acts designed to make a person subordinate and/or dependent by isolating them from sources of support, [...] and regulating their everyday behaviour.
- 'Coercive behaviour' means an act or a pattern of acts of assault, threats, humiliation and intimidation or other abuse that is used to harm, punish, or frighten the victim. (Justice 2014: S3)

Rob's behaviour is also eloquently illustrated in the Duluth Power and Control wheel with its focus on coercion, threats, intimidation, emotional and economic abuse, isolation, the use of children in these, and the use of male privilege (IFVS 2015). The 'Using Emotional Abuse' and 'Using Isolation' sections of this seem particularly relevant:

- Putting her down
- Making her feel bad about herself
- Calling her names
- Making her think she's crazy
- Playing mind games
- Making her feel guilty

- Controlling what she does, who she sees and talks to, what she reads, where she goes, limiting her outside involvement [...].

This is also the basis of 'Coercive Control', now defined in UK law in the Serious Crime Act 2015, and which should be dealt with as part of adult and/or child safeguarding and public protection procedures.

Violence and abuse is often seen as something that just happens to women, perpetrated by men. However I would argue that it must now be recognized (as it is in British law), that such abuse and control is perpetrated against both men and women by partners of either sex – this situation could equally have been Shula controlling Alistair, or between Adam and Ian.

So, through listening, and in discussing this in our supervision sessions and through online discussions, which I will look at shortly, my student will have learned about abusive relationships, and how professionals, friends and family can be fooled and indeed become inadvertently collusive with the abuse. He will have learned about the impact on children (and considered whether we would carry out a pre-birth assessment in this case), and come to understand victims' perspectives, the dynamics of violence – and also learned about legal and policy contexts and relevant procedures.

Learning from Narrative

Use of dramatic narratives in social work education is a way of teaching and learning that is not widely used, but has much potential. One of the outcomes of engaging with dramatic narrative is that our relationships with the dramatis personae can be intense – as I'm sure we may all recognize from our own listening habits – and that this can bring out strong feelings; developing such empathy can enable readers or listeners to relate themes from the narrative to their own experiences, and this then enables reflection on both themes and experience.

As Helen Walmsley-Johnson wrote in *The New Statesman*, 'Storylines like this are really best covered by the soap genre because they allow an almost real-time development of the plot' (Walmsley-Johnson 2016). Rob and Helen's relationship is being shown to us in a way that truly does reflect the experience of others, as messages on social media in the last few months have made increasingly clear. It is the sort of concerning situation where social workers, were they to become involved, would never see the full dynamics during their visits, and would more than likely meet hostility or minimization of concerns, as indeed Helen's family did. Irvine et al.'s (2015) research found that students wanted to learn more about the perspectives of service users who might be critical of social work intervention, in order to develop more effective skills in working with them. It is important to remember, however, that insights into the real life experience of a particular issue can not necessarily be generalized to all people experiencing something similar. We cannot say for certain that all couples where one is controlled by the other experience the same as Helen and Rob, but we can start to recognize patterns that fit certain common behavioural traits.

The Role of Discussion in Developing Learning

Blended learning – using online methods as well as more traditional class-room teaching – is well established across Higher Education. The use of online discussion, if well designed and managed, is widely understood to be an effective online teaching method in terms of meeting students' diverse learning needs and styles (Madoc-Jones and Parrott 2005), and in creating communities of learning (Gillingham 2009) and communities of practice (Moore 2008). The use of a discussion forum enables students to explore difficult issues whilst respecting the privacy of their own histories – this enables both self-development (in understanding the viewpoints of others) and the development of professional competencies, the use of 'self' in practice, and empathy in particular, which has been shown by Forrester et al. (2008) and others to be a crucial factor in good engagement and promoting change with service users in complex situations.

Good discussions can of course take place in the classroom, but time constraints can limit the possibilities for exploring understanding, values and related skills (Chaumba 2015). The on-line medium allows students to explore 'at a distance', in spaces that they feel safe in, without the need to be literally face to face with their audience. Discussions in social media certainly appear to enable this openness; however in the interests of student confidentiality and privacy, online discussion can easily be facilitated on university online workspaces such as Blackboard or Moodle.

A Final Point

I have used online discussion groups to develop student 'communities of practice' (Burrows 2010) and would agree with Moore's (2009) point that central to understanding communities of practice is viewing work and learning as social activities. Working together, people learn from each other and develop a shared purpose, a common way of thinking and talking and eventually share a sense of mutual identity.

This model appears to have moved from professional practice into public social action through the power of social media. I am a member of the Archers Appreciation group on Facebook, and I cannot end this chapter without a mention of the initiative set up by Paul Trueman, another member, who, following ongoing group discussion of domestic abuse, set up a Just Giving page to raise money for the charity Refuge, with the aim of helping 'all the Helens, male and female' as one giver described it. This raised over £40,000 in a mere six days, and by June 2016 had reached over £130,000; the comments and tweets are testament to the public raising of awareness of domestic abuse. People have shared their own experiences, have shared how Helen and Rob's story has changed their perceptions and values and helped them to understand what needs to be done to help victims of abuse escape.

References

Burrows, H. (2010). 'Engaging Dinosaurs: An Experiment in E-Learning on a Post-Qualifying Programme'. RDI4 Action learning, University of Bradford, 10 December 2010.

Chaumba, J. (2015). 'Using Blogs to Stimulate Reflective Thinking in a Human Behavior Course', *Social Work Education* 34.4: 377–90.

Clapp, S. (2016). 'The 10 Best *Archers* Storylines', *The Guardian*, 22 January 2016 <http://www.theguardian.com/tv-and-radio/2016/jan/22/the-10-best-archers-storylines-rob-helen> accessed 22 January 2016.

Domakin, A. (2015). 'The Importance of Practice Learning in Social Work: Do We Practice What We Preach?', *Social Work Education* 34.4: 399–413.

Forrester, D., S. Kershaw, H. Moss and L. Hughes (2008). 'Communication Skills in Child Protection: How Do Social Workers Talk to Parents?', *Child & Family Social Work* 13.1: 41–51.

Gillingham, P. (2009). 'Ghosts in the Machine: Student Participation and Grade Attainment in a Web-Assisted Social Work Course', *Social Work Education* 28.4: 423–35.

Institute for Family Violence Studies (IFVS) (2015). 'The Power and Control Wheel' <http://familyvio.csw.fsu.edu/online-dv-tutorials/cbt-wic-staff/chapter-1/the-power-and-control-wheel/> accessed 7 February 2016.

Irvine, J., J. Molyneux and M. Gillman (2015). '"Providing a Link with the Real World": Learning from the Student Experience of Service User and Carer Involvement in Social Work Education', *Social Work Education* 34.2: 138–50.

Justice (2014). *Practice Direction 12J – Child Arrangements & Contact Order: Domestic Violence and Harm* <https://www.justice.gov.uk/courts/procedure-rules/family/practice_directions/pd_part_12j> accessed 13 January 2016.

Madoc-Jones, I., and L. Parrott (2005). 'Virtual Social Work Education: Theory and Experience', *Social Work Education* 24.7: 755–68.

Moore, B. (2008). 'Using Technology to Promote Communities of Practice (CoP) in Social Work Education', *Social Work Education* 27.6: 592–600.

The College of Social Work (TCSW) (2012). *The Practitioner Capabilities Framework* <https://www.basw.co.uk/resource/?id=1137> accessed 7 February 2016.

Walmsley-Johnson, H. (2016). 'Helen's Story of Abuse in *The Archers* Reminds Me of My Own – So I'm Willing Her To Leave', *The New Statesman* <http://www.newstatesman.com/politics/feminism/2016/02/helen-s-story-abuse-archers-reminds-me-my-own-so-i-m-willing-her-leave> accessed 2 February 2016.

Review by Kirsty Miller, Willow Farm, Ambridge, Borsetshire

OMG! I wish I'd known about this before, it makes so much sense. Rob just seemed so … nice … so charming … and Helen kept on saying she was fine, and they were so happy. And Pat said I shouldn't be worrying, it was just Helen being Helen as usual … I just feel I let her down, what with being away for so long, maybe if her brother Tom hadn't left me at the altar … If he hadn't done that, if I'd still been here, maybe I'd have seen through Rob earlier and I could have helped her see what he was doing to her before it got to where it did. It never occurred to me that they would both hide what was going on, that we couldn't see what went on behind closed doors … Don't get me wrong, I don't blame Helen, I see now what she was going through, she got so she didn't believe in herself anymore. I wish I'd seen all the stuff on Facebook! I didn't know about coercive control until the woman at the helpline told me about it when I rang up to find out if there was anything I could do to help Helen – even then I think she thought I was talking about myself – but it was a good suggestion to give her a burn phone, I hope the police know if she used it to call the helpline herself. Helen shouldn't have done what she did, but the bastard deserved what he got!

CARENZA LEWIS AND CLEMENCY COOPER

Dig *The Archers*: What Community Archaeological Excavations Can Achieve in Places like Ambridge

In setting The Archers *in lowland England, BBC Radio 4 scriptwriters planted their dramatis personae into an ancient landscape inhabited by humans over millennia. Here, rural settlements of the sort epitomized by Ambridge, with its timber-framed cottages, village green and medieval parish church, may have existed for hundreds of years (Christie and Stamper 2012; Lewis et al. 1997; Rippon 2008; Rowley 1978; Taylor 1983). However, little is usually known about the long-term development of such places, which is often remarkably dynamic. But while the remains of abandoned historic villages have long excited both scholarly and public interest (Taylor 2012), currently occupied rural settlements (CORS) are often overlooked as historic sites, not least by their inhabitants who may be more concerned with present and future concerns than past histories. Even in CORS where written documents have been researched by active local history societies (which Ambridge, rather surprisingly, lacks), it is usually presumed that any pre-modern archaeological evidence will have been destroyed by later construction and is in any case inaccessible under existing houses and gardens. However, recent research has not only shown that copious archaeological evidence does survive under such places (e.g. Audouy and Chapman 2009) which prioritizes them for academic research but has also demonstrated the wide range of benefits such projects can deliver within and beyond rural communities such as Ambridge. Further, residents of rural communities such as Ambridge are increasingly recognized as being able to make significant contributions to research by carrying out archaeological projects such as those discussed here (Hedge and Nash 2016).*

Digging Ambridge

Excavating within the sort of places which Ambridge epitomizes requires appropriate techniques, as with today's rural villages, hamlets and small towns, appropriate locations, such as greens (if present), parks or gardens. A technique which is both feasible and effective is the excavation of one million square 'test pits' (TPs) (Gerrard and Aston 2007: 244–61; Cooper and Priest 2003; Lewis 2007). Being small in area and depth, thus neat and quick to complete, test pits can be sited in domestic gardens (see Figure 7) where larger, more disruptive excavation may not be permitted by property owners. Each pit produces new archaeological evidence for the history of its individual site, and when the data from many pits excavated within the same village are combined and mapped, the resulting patterns can not only reconstruct the often turbulent development of individual communities (Gerrard and Aston 2012) but when aggregated with other villages can throw new light on major historic phenomena such as the Roman Empire (Cooper 2013) and the Black Death (Lewis 2016).

Test pit excavation within CORS is impossible without community involvement, a necessity which is in fact a virtue, as has been demonstrated in eastern England where over two thousand test pits have been excavated in more than sixty rural communities under the aegis of a single academic director (Lewis 2014). Here, local hands-on participation has not only inspired and enthused residents from all backgrounds who take part in excavations which are literally right on their doorstep (Lewis 2015), but also raised academic aspirations amongst more than five thousand teenagers through university-led Higher Education Field Academy (HEFA) courses during which they complete a test pit excavation as part of a wider educational programme (Catling 2010; Lewis 2014; HEFA 2016; see Figure 7). Ambridge represents an archetypal English rural community, so exploring its role contributing to and benefiting from such projects can exemplify this elsewhere.

One route to involvement in test pit excavation is through local historical societies (Hey 2012; Riden 1998). Although Ambridge, somewhat surprisingly, does not have one, someone like Jennifer Aldridge, with her longstanding (although recently dormant) interest in local history (Aldridge and Tregorran 1981) will pick up such an enquiry enthusiastically and quickly involve like-minded neighbours, typified in Ambridge by veterans of the 1980s Ambridge parish survey (ibid.: 1–3), Shula Archer (now Hebden Lloyd), Caroline Bone (now Sterling) and Pat Archer. News spreads quickly through local social networks, whether by word of mouth, notices in village shops, or announcements in church. Given the appeal

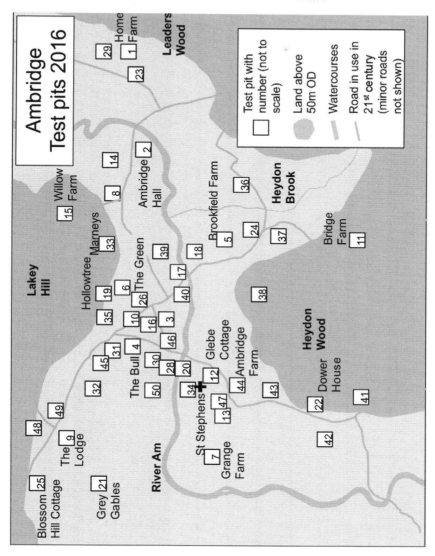

Figure 7: Ambridge test pits 2016.
All images in this chapter © Carenza Lewis 2016.

of supporting a good cause which might also uncover some historic finds
it is usually easy for local coordinators to find volunteers to offer their
gardens. Communities can also develop their own test pit projects. At
Pirton, Hertfordshire, more than one hundred pits have been completed
since the first HEFA in 2007 (Pirton Local History Group 2011), while
at places such as Reeth, Yorkshire, the excavation of fifty pits excavated by
local residents in three villages was funded by the Heritage Lottery Fund
(Dennison-Edson and Mills 2014). In somewhere like Ambridge, hands-on
residents such as Joe and Eddie Grundy would be immensely interested in
such a treasure hunt; while some residents like Lynda Snell, or a vociferous Sabrina Thwaite, may be dubious about allowing a load of unknown
teenagers from as far away as Felpersham, Borchester and Birmingham to
excavate in their immaculate gardens, but would happily volunteer Robert
or Richard for the community-driven project.

Knowledgeable residents such as Jennifer, Shula or Pat sometimes
suspect that little that is new will be revealed by excavating somewhere like
Ambridge where a detailed parish survey has been completed (Aldridge and
Tregorran 1981). However, test pit excavation elsewhere shows this not to be
the case, with medieval, Roman or prehistoric activity often unexpectedly
present or, indeed, absent. At Cottenham, Cambridgeshire, for example,
an area which the HEFA team were repeatedly assured had only ever been
orchards before its existing nineteenth- and twentieth-century houses were
built revealed a continuous pottery sequence running from the Roman
period to the late medieval. Likewise, in the seaside village of Walberswick,
Suffolk, a lane devoid of known settlement until the late nineteenth century proved to be densely inhabited in the centuries leading up to the Black
Death. Conversely, at Carleton Rode, Norfolk, more than ten pits around
the thirteenth-century church produced virtually no medieval finds, with
the dispersed Anglo-Saxon and medieval settlements shown to lie half a mile
away. All this data lies well beyond the radar of historical documentation.

Test pit excavations in Ambridge would certainly deliver new knowledge. The exact details of these are invariably unpredictable, and especially so
in Ambridge whose geographical location is somewhat imprecisely known.
Inkberrow in Worcestershire is the main claimant to the 'real Ambridge'

throne, but rival contender Rippingale lies in Lincolnshire. These counties lie in different historic settlement sub-provinces (Roberts and Wrathmell 2000) so confirming the location of Ambridge is crucial to understanding it (see Perkins in this volume for the challenges regarding this). But maps of Ambridge (Magnetic North 2000) show a hilly terrain with a dispersed settlement pattern in the nineteenth century, lacking a green and with scattered farms and homesteads strung out long winding lanes. This form of settlement is characteristic of the Severn and Avon Vales in Worcestershire (Roberts and Wrathmell 2000: 55–60; Roberts and Wrathmell 2002: 4–10) rather than South Lincolnshire (ibid.: 48–9).

Worcestershire has seen little test pit excavation within CORS (Hurst 2014: 279) which could be used to predict the results of test pit excavations in Ambridge (although this usefully highlights how valuable work in this area of the UK would be). Although local, there have been some very useful parish surveys involving documentary research and field-walking in Pendock and Hanbury (Dyer 1990, 1991), and a small number of test pits dug in Droitwich, Wychbold and Hanley (Hurst 2014). These can be compared with larger numbers of test pit excavations elsewhere in parishes with dispersed settlements (such as Carlton Rode, Norfolk; Clavering, Essex; and Manude, Essex).

Mapping the finds from Ambridge test pits (see Figures 8–12) reveals its historic development. To summarize the detailed analysis (Lewis forthcoming), thinly scattered prehistoric activity (see Figure 8) over thousands of years favours the south-facing valley sides in the north of the parish, including a possible Bronze Age cremation near the river (TP 2) and Iron Age settlement (TP 6). In the Roman period (see Figure 8), doubtless encouraged by the new Roman road, the area north of the River Am becomes much more densely settled with woodland to its south cleared for new sites at TP 1 and TP 36. This growth reverses in the early Anglo-Saxon period (see Figure 9), with nearly all former settlement (bar TP 48 and possibly TP 1) apparently abandoned. In the late Anglo-Saxon period (see Figure 9) new sites, small in size, appear on the banks of the River Am (TP 6/34) and in the south of the parish (TP 1 and 37). Dramatic growth in the High Medieval period (see Figure 10) sees these proliferate into chains

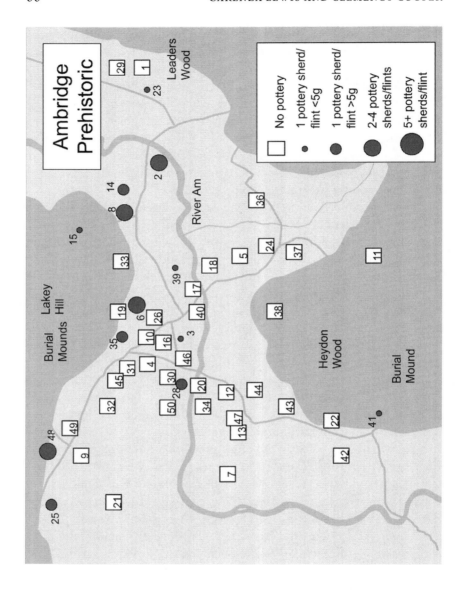

Ambridge
Prehistoric

No pottery

1 pottery sherd/
flint <5g

1 pottery sherd/
flint >5g

2-4 pottery
sherds/flints

5+ pottery
sherds/flint

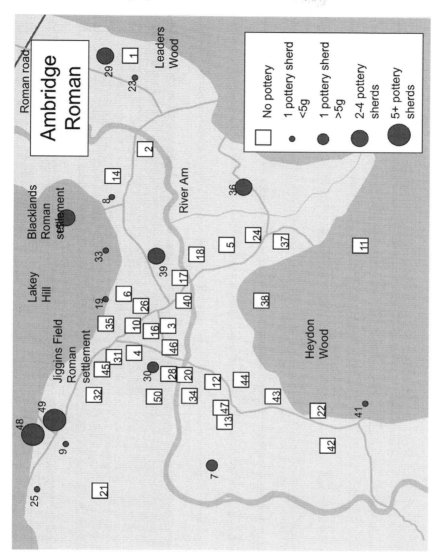

Figure 8: Prehistoric (800,000 BC–43 AD) finds in Ambridge (left). Roman (43 AD–410 AD) finds in Ambridge (right).

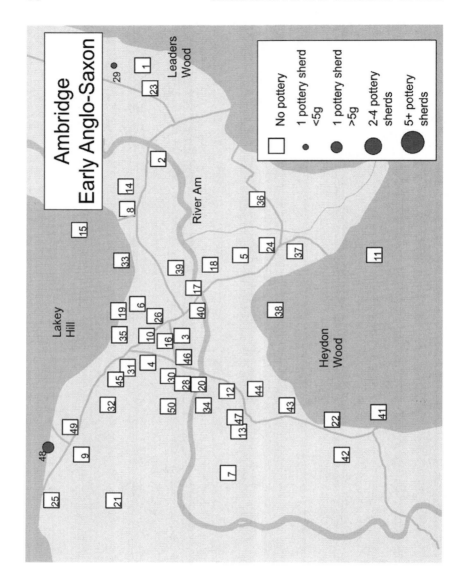

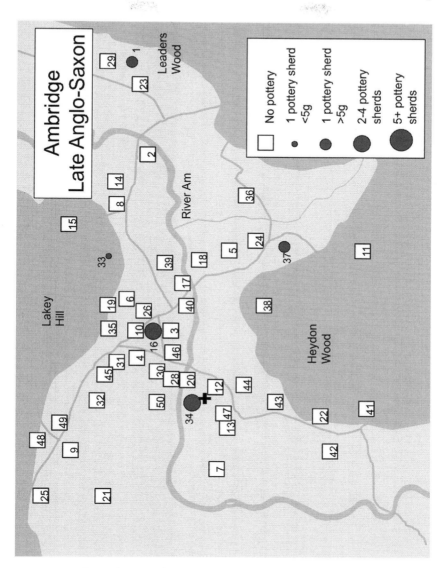

Figure 9: Early Anglo-Saxon (mid-fifth–eighth century AD) finds in Ambridge (left).
Late Anglo-Saxon (ninth–eleventh century AD) finds in Ambridge (right).

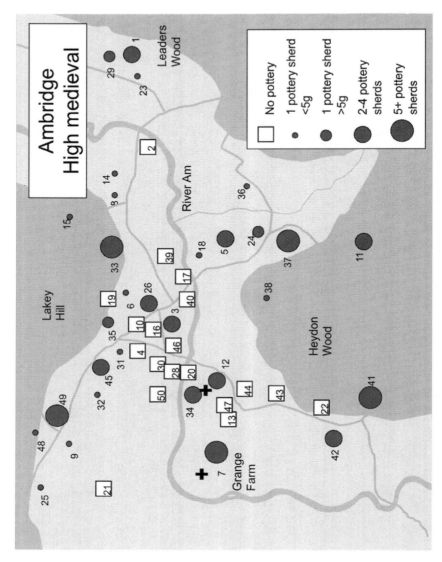

Figure 10: High Medieval (twelfth–mid-fourteenth century AD) finds in Ambridge.

of dispersed farmsteads strung out along lanes across the lower-lying land (TP 3/5/12/26/33/34/42/49), interspersed with manured arable fields indicated by smaller amounts of pottery (TP 6/8/9/14/15/18/23/25/31/36/48) and encroaching onto higher former woodland (TP 1/11/37/41). Catastrophic decline after the Black Death (see Figure 11) sees many outlying farms apparently abandoned (TP 17/11/37/41/42/49/33) as settlement focuses in on the lower valley side near the church (TP 4/12/26/30). Eventual recovery (see Figure 11), stimulated by the Industrial Revolution and the turn-piking of the Borchester-Worcester road, saw the former dispersed settlement pattern readopted, complemented with a larger village arranged along lanes mostly north of the church (4/10/26/28/30/31). Victorian infilling (see Figure 12) and ribbon development along the Hollerton Road (TP 22/43/44) is encouraged by the railway station at Hollerton Junction. Overall, Ambridge's development appears similar to nearby Hanbury (Dyer 1991), with which it has close connections.

However, the benefits of community test pit projects extend even beyond the contribution they make to historical and archaeological knowledge. Members of host communities benefit through becoming better connected with their shared place-based past, developing new skills and knowledge about their heritage and by forging new friendships in the present (Lewis 2015). Feedback shows 'meeting people' is the most highly appreciated aspect of the activity, ranked above even 'finding things'. Excavating together requires teamwork and is enjoyable and satisfying, creating lasting bonds. This is the case even in villages where one might expect everyone to know everyone already, such as Ambridge. Historically minded local coordinators such as Jennifer, Pat or Shula typically wish to ensure that the distribution of pit sites include all parts of the village (in order to increase its research value), leading them to recruit in streets and closes (such as Glebelands and Grange Spinney) where they may have virtually no existing social contact. Beyond the immediate community, the social contact afforded by bringing HEFA teenagers to excavate in the gardens of rural residents, significant numbers of whom may be elderly and isolated, can be immensely positive (Lewis 2014). The young people appreciate being welcomed and trusted, while the hosts enjoy the youthful company in an intergenerational exchange which benefits from being able to develop in the

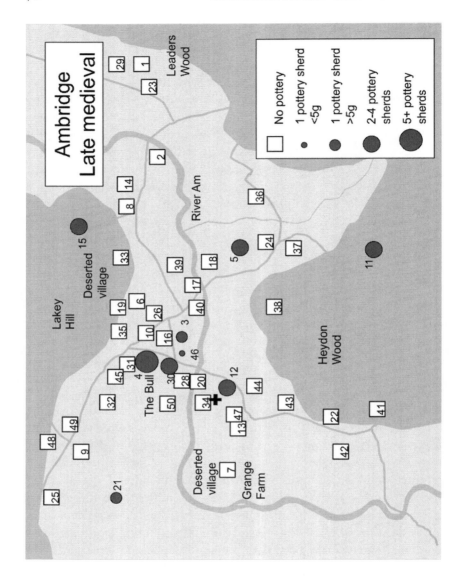

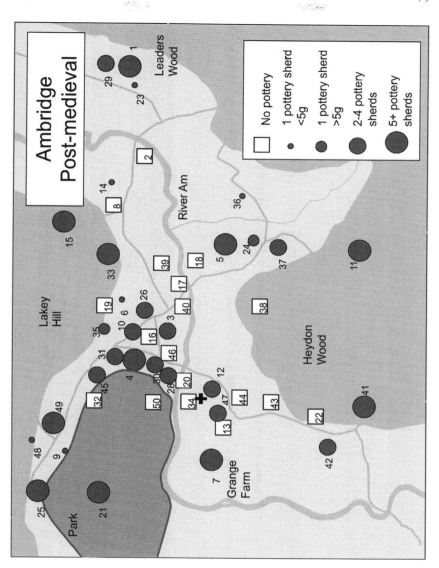

Figure 11:   Late Medieval (mid-fourteenth–mid-sixteenth century AD)
finds in Ambridge (left). Post-Medieval (late sixteenth–late eighteenth
century AD) finds in Ambridge (right).

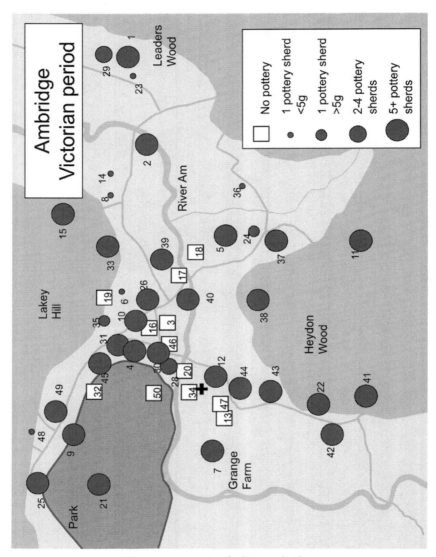

Figure 12: Victorian finds in Ambridge.

informal setting of an archaeological excavation, rather than structured as a formal social engagement. And finally, of course, there is the impact on teenagers who take part in HEFA courses. In eastern England, more than five thousand teenagers have completed HEFA since 2005 and feedback shows more than eighty per cent leave with their learning skills, confidence and academic aspirations all significantly raised, an impact which is both strong and enduring (Lewis 2014). This is helping tackle inequalities in progression to university by young people which is still unacceptably low in many rural areas.

It is thus clear that rural communities such as Ambridge, with their historic roots, their deeply embedded social networks and their shallow-buried garden-sited archaeology, can make possible the sort of archaeological projects that not only create new knowledge and enrich lives in the present, but also build skills and aspirations for the future, with impacts radiating far beyond the rural communities who host them.

Acknowledgements

The excavations discussed here have been funded by Aimhigher, The Higher Education Funding Council for England, English Heritage, the University of Cambridge, the University of Lincoln, the Heritage Lottery Fund, the Arts and Humanities Research Council, Arts Council England and several smaller bodies: their support is gratefully acknowledged. Literally thousands of people have had an essential involvement and for reasons of space thanks must be given to them anonymously, remembering especially those who took part in test pit excavations or permitted these on their property and those who helped online with Ambridge research. The excavations were directed by Carenza Lewis, supervised by Catherine Ranson and coordinated by Clemency Cooper and Laure Bonner. Special thanks are also due to Jessica Rippengal, Paul Blinkhorn, John Newman, Andrew Rogerson, and the management committee of the McDonald Institute for Archaeological Research at the University of Cambridge for their valuable support.

References

Aldridge, J., and J. Tregorran (1981). *Ambridge: An English Village Through the Ages*. London: Methuen.

Catling, C. (2010). 'Test Pits and Teaching' in *Current Archaeology* 239: 30–35.

Audouy, M., and A. Chapman (eds) (2009). *Raunds: The Origin and Growth of a Midland Village AD 450–1500*. Oxford: Oxbow Books.

Cooper, C. (2013). 'Continuity and Change in Context: Evidence for the Roman to Medieval Transition from the HEFA CORS Project'. Unpublished MSc thesis, University of Oxford.

Cooper, N., and P. Priest (2003). 'Sampling a Medieval Village in a Day: Annual Report', *Medieval Settlement Research Group* 18: 53–6.

Crowther, S., and V. Clarke (2012). 'Worcestershire Historic Landscape Characterisation'. *Worcester: Worcestershire County Council* <http://gis.worcestershire.gov.uk/website/hlcpublishing/documents/SWR21534.pdf> accessed 10 June 2016.

Dennison-Edson, P., and A. Mills (2014). 'The Swaledale Big Dig', *Forum: Journal of the Council for British Archaeology Yorkshire* 4: 65–76.

Dyer, C. (1990). 'Dispersed Settlements in Medieval England: A Case Study of Pendock, Worcestershire', *Medieval Archaeology* 34: 97–121.

Dyer, C. (1991). *Hanbury: Settlement and Society in a Woodland Landscape*. Leicester: Leicester University Press.

Gerrard, C., and M. Aston (2007). 'The Shapwick Project, Somerset: A Rural Landscape Explored', *Society for Medieval Archaeology* Monograph 25. Leeds: Society for Medieval Archaeology.

Hedge, R., and A. Nash (2016). 'Assessing the Value of Community-Generated Historic Environment Research'. Report for *Historic England* <https://historicengland.org.uk/images-books/publications/assessing-value-of-community-generated-historic-environment-research/> accessed 16 June 2016.

HEFA (2016). *Higher Education Field Academies* <http://www.access.arch.cam.ac.uk/schools/hefa> accessed 27 June 2016.

Hey, D. (ed.) (2010). *The Oxford Companion to Family and Local History*. Oxford: Oxford University Press (2nd edn, paperback).

Historic England (2015). 'Heritage Counts' (unpublished report).

Hurst, D. (2014). 'Test Pit Digging in Worcestershire in Currently Occupied Rural Settlements', *Transactions of the Worcestershire Archaeological Society* 24: 279–81.

Lewis, C. (forthcoming). 'Archaeological Test Pit Excavations in Ambridge, Borsetshire 2016', *Past Investigations of Cultural Heritage Environments*.

Lewis, C. (2016). 'Disaster Recovery? New Archaeological Evidence from Eastern England for the Impact of the "Calamitous" 14th century', *Antiquity* 90.351: 777–97 <http://dx.doi.org/10.15184/aqy.2016.69>.

Lewis, C. (2015). 'Archaeological Excavation and Deep Mapping in Historic Rural Communities', *Humanities* 4: 393–417; DOI: 10.3390/h4030393.

Lewis, C. (2014a). 'The Power of Pits: Archaeology, outreach and research in Living Landscapes', in K. Boyle, R. Rabett and C. Hunt (eds), *Living in the Landscape*. Cambridge: McDonald Institute for Archaeological Research Monograph: 321–38.

Lewis, C. (2014b). '"Cooler than a Trip to Alton Towers": Assessing the Impact of the Higher Education Field Academy 2005–2013', *Public Archaeology* 13.4: 295–322.

Lewis, C. (2007). 'New Avenues in the Investigation of Currently-Occupied Rural Settlements: Preliminary Results from the Higher Education Field Academy', *Medieval Archaeology* 51: 133–64.

Magnetic North (2000). *Ambridge and Borchester District: The Definitive Map of The Archers on BBC Radio 4* (Dorchester: Magnetic North for the BBC).

Moshenska, G., and S. Dhanjal (eds) (2012). *Community Archaeology: Themes, Methods and Practices*. Oxford: Oxbow Books.

Pirton Local History Group (2011). Archaeological project <http://www.pirton-history.org.uk/archaeology-landscape/archaeological-project/> accessed 27 June 2016.

Riden, P. (1998). *Local History: A Handbook for Beginners*. Cardiff: Merton Press (2nd edn).

Roberts, B. K., and S. Wrathmell (2000). *An Atlas of Rural Settlement in England*. London: English Heritage.

Roberts, B. K., and S. Wrathmell (2002). *Region and Place*. London: English Heritage.

Slater, T., and P. Jarvis (eds) (1982). *Field and Forest: An Historical Geography of Warwickshire and Worcestershire*. [n. pub.] [n.p].

Skeates, R., C. McDavid and J. Carman (2012). *The Oxford Handbook of Public Archaeology*. Oxford: Oxford University Press.

Watt, S. (ed.) (2011). *The Archaeology of the West Midlands: A Framework for Research*. Oxford: Oxbow Books.

Review by Jennifer Aldridge (transcript of interview conducted via Skype)

(Note: In the pre-proof copy of this chapter supplied to Jennifer for review, paragraph six was inexplicably absent. This error has been corrected in this published version).

Well, when I first saw the email from the University of Cambridge and University of Lincoln requesting to dig in Ambridge I admit I thought it was a joke, but then I saw online what's been done in other places – remarkable. The HEFA was the first revelation – some of those schools have a terrible reputation, but the children were all so polite and worked so hard although not one of them had done anything like that before – they got so much out of it. Everyone loved our community dig, and not just for Jill's end-of-day cakes! Clarrie was so happy to see Eddie, Ed and Will working together, digging Carol's (TP 12) and Peggy's (TP 9) pits as well as their own (TP 7/26). It's a shame Tony's back let him down, but Pat certainly enjoyed working out her frustrations – I can't believe how hard she hit that clay at Bridge Farm (TP 11). It's so intriguing to see how much Ambridge has changed in the past. I'm surprised how shocked I've felt seeing that Home Farm (TP 1/23/29) was abandoned after the Black Death – it brings it alive, somehow (although if I'm honest I'm getting a little tired of Susan going on about all 'her' (i.e. Neil's) prehistoric finds (TP 6) – 'so unexpected from such a new house', as she keeps pointing out). And it's very gratifying to hear 'our' dig will be officially published – in the prestigious *Journal of Past Investigations into Cultural Heritage Environments*, no less! Everyone is now keen to do so much more!

PHILIPPA BYRNE

The Medieval World of *The Archers*, William Morris and the Problem with Class Struggle

Social relations in Ambridge are best understood if we consider it as a model medieval village – the kind of medieval village imagined by the Victorian author William Morris (1834–96). The most important conflicts in Ambridge in recent years have been the confrontation between 'modernity' and 'tradition', between those who defend the dignity of labour and those who value technology above all else. This chapter first explains the concept of 'anti-utilitarian medievalism' (Fradenberg 1997), and then considers how it applies to events in Ambridge. This paradigm allows us to appreciate how issues as diverse as Fallon and Emma's Ambridge Tea Room, the evil of Rob Titchener, and Route B are linked together as part of a wider 'medieval' narrative.

Introduction

One way of explaining how Ambridge 'works' is to invoke the class system: Aldridges at the top, Archers in the middle, Grundys at the bottom, and Horrobins still further below, the true *lumpenproletariat*. Neil Kinnock memorably claimed the programme should be renamed *The Grundys and Their Oppressors* (Hendy 2007). But there are problems with this neat model – not least the belief that British society has now supposedly transcended notions of class, and the fact that class struggle is probably not meet matter for 7.02pm on BBC Radio 4.

There are obvious differences in wealth and status across Ambridge, but they are rarely the central theme of episodes. *The Archers* is notoriously reticent in discussing money (how much did Jennifer's new kitchen cost?) and Emma's desperately sad trip to the foodbank, for example, was never set in a social or structural context of the struggle of the under-employed or low-paid families. Much of the time, different 'classes' rub along quite happily – and strangely – together: Jim and Jazzer, Carol and Bert.

Position and status are important, but it is work which defines the community in Ambridge and attitudes to work which distinguish those who are part of the community from those who stand outside it. It is for that reason I suggest that *The Archers* most resembles a romanticized vision of the 'medieval' village.

The particular vision of a medieval village on display in *The Archers* is strikingly similar to that sketched out by the group of Christian Socialist thinkers associated with the later Victorian Arts and Crafts movement and, in particular, with the author, artist and social revolutionary William Morris. This is not to claim that the editors and scriptwriters have consciously decided to create in Ambridge a model medieval village, but that Ambridge's storylines, when put together, embody an argument about the Middle Ages. The forces of good, represented by 'medieval ideals' of the dignity of labour and community, are pitted against the forces of evil, represented by a rootless modernity which desires only profit, and places no value on toil, craft or experience.

Sadly, I cannot claim to be the first person to talk about a 'medieval' Ambridge. That landmark work, Lynda Snell's *Heritage of Ambridge* (1997), notes that the Grundys trace their descent to the Vikings – accounting for their healthy disrespect for authority – and that the Archers' own ancestors were literal archers at the Battle of Agincourt in 1415, leading the charge in the Hundred Years' War. Next to Grange Farm, allegedly, is a deserted medieval village. The wassailing ceremony – a ceremonial performance at which songs are sung to apple trees to wish for a healthy new crop – was introduced to Ambridge and the Grundy Orchard only in 2016 but may possibly represent an Anglo-Saxon tradition (Baskervill 1920). There is, therefore, a recognizably medieval backdrop to Ambridge.

Moreover, Jim Lloyd, Ambridge's unofficial historian, serves to emphasize this medieval context. Jim's speciality – the classics and ancient Rome – is a topic that he frequently invokes in conversation (see Samantha Walton's contribution to this volume). Jim laments that the 'glories' of Rome are long gone: Ambridge folk cannot remember their dates and no longer know their Latin. Jim even threatens to read, in Latin, the work of Virgil – the great poet of Roman imperialism – at Linda's Christmas show. Jim, harking back to Rome, frames Ambridge: post-Roman; pre-industrial; engaged in a struggle with modernity.

William Morris's Middle Ages

William Morris set out a very specific vision of the Middle Ages, a vision that can be termed 'anti-utilitarian medievalism' (Alexander 2007). Morris was a radical social reformer, who looked around at the modern industrialized world with horror. In *The Earthly Paradise*, he describes the industrial world: 'six counties overhung with smoke [...] the snorting steam and piston smoke, the spreading of the hideous town' (Morris 1870). In Morris's view, the development of 'industry' had removed craft and skill from labour, positioning labourers as mere machines. This was, for Morris, the inevitable consequence of a utilitarian approach to human society: a civilization measuring only output and profit, caring little for the process of creation.

Morris did not simply catalogue the woes of the industrial worker, but also sketched out a solution: to return to the early Middle Ages, a time when social distinctions were less stark, before power was less concentrated, and labour had inherent dignity (Harris 1984). Morris believed that social inequality had arrived later in history, in the form of lords who profited from peasants' labour without themselves doing any work (Peteri 2009). This creeping development of social inequality is illustrated in his 1888 work *A Dream of John Ball*, in which the Victorian narrator travels to the Peasants' Revolt of 1381. The leader of the peasants, the eponymous John Ball, explains to the traveller that the ideal community is one based on 'fellowship', wherein the dignity and value of each individual's labour is recognized. There he explains that 'fellowship is heaven, and lack of fellowship is hell [...] the deeds that ye do upon the earth [...] shall live on and on for ever' (Morris 1888). Morris articulates an ideal of community solidarity which is both central to life in Ambridge and forever threatening to come unstuck at moments of crisis in the village.

Those values of skilled labour and fellowship had been given form in medieval art and architecture. The Middle Ages, unlike the modern world, had produced beautiful things, through careful and labour-intensive craft. Morris contrasted the 'pleasure and exultation' produced by traditional methods of craft with 'the meanness of the modern street and its petty commercialism' (Morris 1996).

This brief overview inevitably flattens out many of the subtleties of Morris's vision, but the key is conflict: a self-supporting community of skilled labourers under attack from rootless utilitarian modernity. This is exactly the sort of conflict we hear played out in Ambridge.

Meaningful Labour, Meaningless Work

A core distinction at the heart of *The Archers* is the difference between 'meaningful labour' and 'meaningless work'. It builds on Morris's belief that humans are happy and at their best when performing fulfilling tasks. The problem is that modern industry does not always recognize the value of their work. This is not as simple as assuming everything 'modern' in Ambridge is corrupt or that everything old is valuable. But this principle is evident in David Archer's plaintive cry when obliged to confront the future of the Brookfield herd: 'We [dairy farmers] used to produce what the country wanted ... now milk is just a commodity'. The traditional link between production, hard work and value has gone. It is at such times that things are most frightening in Ambridge.

By contrast, meaningful labour has a worthy and ennobling character. Consider what might be termed the 'redemption' of Charlie Thomas. When Berrow Farm suffered its plague of botulism, all its modern equipment could not protect its cattle. Instead, Charlie worked unceasingly to try to save his animals, investing not just time, but also love in his labour, cradling sad-eyed calves in his arms as they slowly expired.

The most striking example of the conflict between meaningful labour and meaningless work is Fallon and Emma's tea room. Fallon and Emma represent the 'craftspeople', focused on their upcycling endeavours. It may, perhaps, seem a little strange to apply the label 'medieval', or even 'craft', to their work. While it may not be traditional agricultural labour, it is time-consuming and done with care, and the listener is left with little doubt how much effort goes into the business. The tea room itself is filled with the treasures of the past which the pair attempt lovingly to restore. Fallon and Emma place a definite value on history: they cherish it, and invite the modern world to recognize its inherent value and charm. In that sense, they are emulating the Arts and Crafts movement, and even Morris himself.

The unambiguous villains of Ambridge disdain craft and graft. The idea of labour focused on restoring and preserving the past is in sharp contrast with the way Hazel Woolley makes her money: inviting workmen into Keeper's Cottage, modernizing and ramping up the rent – without ever herself being present. Hazel has no interest in the details of labour, only in the profit it can provide. A similar, although less serious, conflict could be traced in relation to Grundy turkeys and Fairbrother geese: the Fairbrothers know how to 'promote' their products, but not pluck their poultry, while Clarrie is an expert in the work of raising birds, but does not know how to sell in the modern marketplace.

Above all, Rob Titchener is the villain who seeks to advance moder-nity. He despised Fallon and Emma's plans for the tea room, describing the contents as 'junk'. Redesigning the Bridge Farm Shop, Rob's preference was for something sleek, modern, possibly with strip-lighting. As Joe Grundy commented, it looked like a place to sell computers. Rob has no time for the objects of Fallon and Emma's restoration work, nor any appreciation of their antiquity – they were just 'chipped crockery' and 'mismatched plates' to him.

The value Rob places on modernity goes hand-in-hand with his dis-dain for labour. This was most obvious in his relationship with Helen: first forcing her into a wholly unnecessary job-share and then removing her from the shop entirely. But the same attitude to labour is also glimpsed in relation to other characters: Rob scorned the workmen at Bridge Farm, and made a threatening phone call to an electrician who failed to keep an appointment. Rob's criticisms implied that tradesmen are interchangeable and easily replaceable. In fact, Rob never praises anyone's work but his own:

he derided Anya, who used to work in the farm shop; he alleged – not just in idle gossip, but when speaking to *The Borsetshire Echo* – that the Berrow Farm plague was directly caused by Charlie Thomas's mismanagement, a blatant untruth.

Rob's presence also disrupts ideas of fellowship – the bedrock on which 'medieval' Ambridge is built. The events of 3 April 2016, including his stabbing by Helen, divided the community. Characters who ought to have shown 'fellowship' with Helen, the victim of Rob's abuse and their friend of many years, instead sided with Rob, her abuser.

Rome and Route B

There is one final recent conflict that demonstrates the ties between Ambridge and a medieval communitarian ideal: *The Archers'* attitude to the Roman Empire. (I concede that it may not seem immediately apparent that Ambridge actually has any particular ideological position vis-à-vis Rome.) Victorian Christian Socialists had a far-from-positive view of the Roman Empire; Morris considered it bureaucratic, cruel and domineering. Rome crushed natural pleasures and communities under its sandal (Morris 1896). For the Middle Ages to achieve freedom, growth and happiness, it had been obliged to throw off Rome, its oppressive organization and its slave culture.

In relation to Rome, Route B – the planned new road that would have run through the centre of Brookfield – must be discussed. This plan represented the wickedest of the wicked forces of utilitarian modernity. It threatened to split the community literally in two. It may have offered utility in shortening the commutes of Borchester and Hollerton inhabitants, but those are far-away towns and people of whom we know nothing. It was, to the residents of Ambridge, wholly destructive, threatening to make the village redundant. Jill's plaintive response to Route B captured the connection between modernity, money and history. Speaking of the field on which the road would be built, she lamented: 'For all we know it's been the same for the last five hundred years, maybe even longer [...]. It's easy to build a new road, all you need is money. But no one can replace a piece of the landscape that's been there for centuries'.

Route B was triumphantly defeated in June 2016, with South Borsetshire District Council opting for a different route, a decision that prompted tears and toasts in The Bull. Who was truly responsible for defeating the proposed road is a matter for debate – as Peter Matthews argues in another chapter in this volume, Lynda Snell perhaps deserves more credit than she receives for halting the diggers. But some sterling work was done by Jennifer in her guise as 'the Boudicca of Borsetshire'. The epithet is significant: the historical Boudicca, while not, strictly speaking, a 'medieval' figure, was the last line in a desperate defence against a vastly richer, vastly better-resourced power which appeared to herald the future but placed no value on tradition or locality.

Jennifer's defence of Ambridge should be set against Justin Elliott's false engagement in the community. Justin offered 'a substantial sum' to restore the village hall, but only on the condition it be named after him. Where Jennifer invests time, Justin invests only money. Despite proclaiming his enjoyment of 'country ways', Justin fundamentally misunderstands how Ambridge works, referring to the Elliotts as a 'brand' he wishes to establish in Ambridge. The problem, I would suggest, is that Justin has fundamentally misread the community and has mistaken it for one based on hierarchy, not fellowship. It remains to be seen whether Justin will 'integrate' into Ambridge, having settled at the Dower House and recognized the need for what might euphemistically be termed Lilian's 'guidance' on country matters. In the long term, then, will Justin turn out to be a Fairbrother goose or a Grundy turkey?

References

Alexander, Michael (2007). *Medievalism: The Middle Ages in Modern England*. London: Yale University Press.

Baskervill, Charles Read (1920). 'Dramatic Aspects of Medieval Folk Festivals', *England in Studies in Philology* 17.1: 19–87.

Fradenberg, Louise (1997). '"So That We May Speak of Them": Enjoying the Middle Ages', *New Literary History* 28.2: 205–30.

Harris, J. (1984). 'William Morris and the Middle Ages'. In J. Banham and J. Harris (eds), *William Morris and the Middle Ages*. Manchester: Manchester University Press: 1–16.

Hendy, David (2007). *A Life on Air: A History of Radio Four*. Oxford: Oxford University Press.

Morris, William (1870). *The Earthly Paradise*. London: F. S. Ellis.

Morris, William (1888). *A Dream of John Ball and A King's Lesson*. London: Reeves and Turner.

Morris, William (1896). *Signs of Change*. London: Longmans, Green and Co.

Morris, William (1996). 'Art and Industry in the Fourteenth Century'. In N. Salmon (ed.), *Morris on History*. Sheffield: Sheffield Academic Press: 90–105.

Peteri, E. (2009). 'Morris' "A King's Lesson": A Hungarian Perspective', *Journal of William Morris Studies* (Winter): 48–55.

Snell, Linda [Boyd, Carol] (1997). *Lynda Snell's Heritage of Ambridge: Her Guide to Archers Country*. London: Virgin Publishing.

Review by Professor Jim Lloyd (University of Stirling, retired), Greenacres, Ambridge, Borsetshire

I have never particularly liked the Middle Ages (can you really trust a civilization which forgets how to produce good wine or to practise indoor plumbing?) but I must confess that I like it even less now if this is the best it can come up with. In my academic life, I conducted myself according to one principle: never trust any article that uses the terrible buzzword 'paradigm' – it marks it out as literary flim-flam of the worst sort. As for those categories of 'tradition' and 'modernity', they are so malleable and broad that you could bend them to mean anything. So I must reject the premise entirely until the argument has been tightened, and, indeed, supported by proper research. If this has been through peer review – something I very much doubt – the process has failed. Disastrously. In fact, it reminds me of a university essay that Kate Aldridge once asked me to look over. I'm afraid this is a classic academic case of overreaching and overthinking. The simple fact of the matter is that I talk about Rome because Roman history is worth talking about. As for my friendship with Jazzer, that is no more the subversion of a class system than the simple fact that he is – I must grudgingly admit – good company. As Cicero said in *De Oratore* (III.36, if the reference is important to you): 'I prefer uneloquent good sense to loquacious folly.' An aphorism to remember when reading this chapter.

CHRIS PERKINS

Mapping Ambridge

It could be argued that the village of Ambridge only exists through the scripts and events narrated in regular broadcasts of the 'everyday story of country folk'. However, iconic locations in the village have a very carefully specified geography. The River Am flows generally from the southwest to the northeast. The Bull is located next to the village green and Grey Gables is on the northwestern edge of Ambridge, on the opposite side of the village to Brookfield etc. Scenes in episodes involving particular characters are related to particular storylines and take place at particular times, and each is crucially located.

This geography of Ambridge is charted in a huge variety of published mapping, as illustrative accompaniments to published spinoff books and as merchandising, but also as compiled and released by fans. These fantasy maps (Balfe 2004; Harmon 2004) reflect changing technologies of production and consumption: the black-and-white diagram characteristic of the 1970s gradually morphs into colour output from mapping software that characterizes publication towards the end of the millennium, and finally has moved towards interactive maps served and shared on websites. It is almost as if the lack of visuals in the programme itself has encouraged a proliferation of maps. Just as maps of real places are many and various so are the maps of Ambridge. Many depict the places where events take place in relation to one another and this chapter explores the geography of Ambridge as revealed in this mapping. I also chart some of the many roles that these maps might play and argue that we ought to interpret them as part of a wider culture beyond the maps themselves. I show how maps come together to reinforce very particular aspects of Ambridge and *The Archers*, but also relate in interesting ways to wider changes in the world of mapping.

The History of Mapping Ambridge

Matt Edney (1993) has persuasively argued that conventional histories of cartography have until relatively recently focused on searching for early maps and exploring the differences between these published images. Academics used to focus on measurement, charting the relative precision

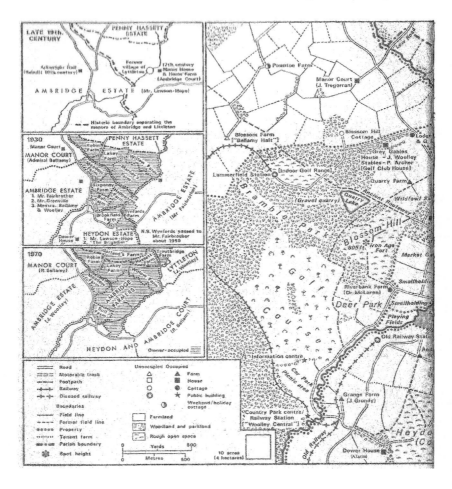

and accuracy of early maps and the progressive 'improvements' in mapping technology. Such an exercise can still be possible with maps of Ambridge. The geography of Ambridge has gradually crystallized during the history of *The Archers*. The earliest published map that I have been able to track down was released in 1975 as a black-and-white line drawing published as the frontispiece to Jock Gallagher's *Twenty-Five Years of The Archers: Who's Who in Ambridge* (see Figure 13). Its style reflects production costs:

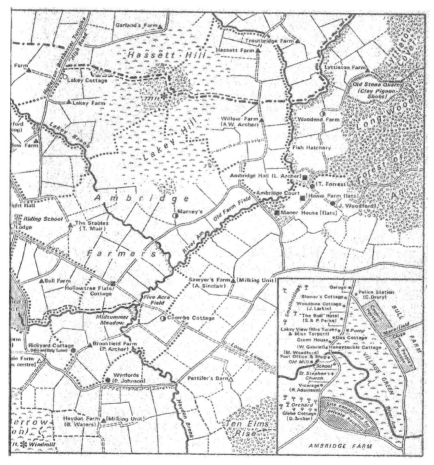

Figure 13: Ambridge in 1975 from Jock Gallagher's *Twenty-Five Years of The Archers: Who's Who in Ambridge* (London: BBC Books, 1975).

colour was prohibitive for publishers and BBC Books presumably saw no need for a sophisticated image. The 1975 detail is interesting. The River Am appears to flow in a bend in the village; Woodbine Cottage is to the north of The Bull; and Honeysuckle Cottage lies adjacent to and on the north bank of the River Am.

Since this original publication a profusion of images has appeared. The level of detail has increased: field names and individual trees are documented in mapping published as part of Anthony Parkin's (1989) *The Archers Book of Farming and the Countryside*. Colour is increasingly now deployed. Mapping can simulate the landscape view of the village as in the 1994 *Archers Addicts Official Map of the Village*. The *Ambridge Panorama* published in 2000 by Magnetic North for the BBC also evokes a green farming landscape, a bird's-eye view reinforcing the pastoral qualities of the programme. Functionality also changes. Mapping on websites can serve as a hyperlink to locations, so you could click on the map of The Bull and access information about the pub and a pictorial record of the building (although the BBC interestingly removed its interactive map of Ambridge in its 2010 redesign of the programme web page).

Claims to authority abound in this cartographic collection and mapping is seen as a medium that persuades by invoking a factual veracity (Perkins 2007). *Ambridge & Borchester District: The Definitive Map of The Archers on BBC Radio 4*, compiled by Magnetic North for the BBC in 2000, epitomizes this trend and is still in print (see Figure 14). This full-colour map is separately published at a scale large enough to show individual buildings, but also incorporates small scale depictions of Borsetshire (centered on Ambridge but also locating Felpersham, Borchester and the surrounding villages such as Edgeley and Penny Hassett, and a larger scale inset map of the centre of Borchester). These three images emulate the style of different official maps and if it feels a bit like an Ordnance Survey map, a motoring atlas and a town plan then this all makes Ambridge all the more real. By 2000 interesting changes seem to have taken place in the village. The course of the River Am has been straightened out, to flow in a broadly easterly direction without the bend in the south of the village, all the way from the edge of the Country Park to beyond the Brookfield Bungalow. Woodbine Cottage appears to have mysteriously moved to the

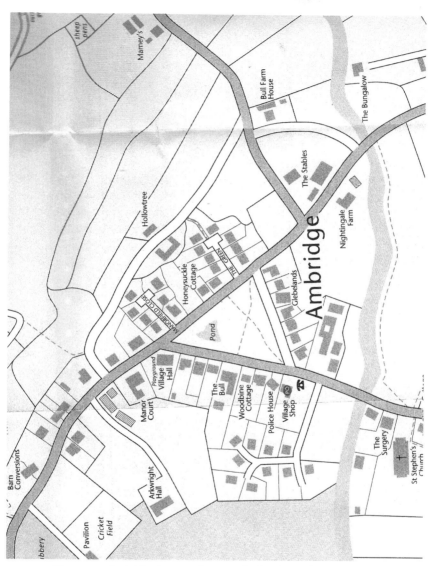

Figure 14: Ambridge in 2000 from *Ambridge & Borchester District:
The Definitive Map of the Archers on BBC Radio 4* (Dorchester:
Magnetic North for the BBC, 2000).

other side of The Bull. Honeysuckle Cottage now appears to the east of
the village green. Perhaps the 1975 map made mistakes? Or maybe changes
reflect events in the twenty-five years' worth of episodes that have elapsed
between the publication of the 1975 and 2000 maps? The village itself has
certainly changed: executive houses on Glebelands have been constructed
for example.

My point, however, is that the apparent precision of the 2000 definitive
map is just as spurious as historians of cartography's charting of progress.
The differences in style of the maps and the apparent changes in the geography of the village speak much more to the changed status of mapping in
1975 and 2000, than they ever do to the apparently neutral status of maps
as depicting a literal changing geography. The look of maps reflects this
cultural difference and their functions change. So instead of bemoaning the
inaccuracy of early mapping of Ambridge we might usefully think about
the politics of mapping and the possibilities that these maps called and call
into play (Dodge, Kitchin and Perkins 2009). That demands exploring
what the maps might be deployed to do.

Using the Maps

Subject to the proviso that mapping Ambridge is an imprecise science
we can nevertheless use maps of the village to work out what takes place
where. We can use the different maps to do a number of practical things
that all maps do. We can use them to chart where Brookfield is in relation
to Hollowtree. On some maps with a scale we can work out how far it is
from Hollerton Junction to Ambridge. We can discover who lives next
door to whom. We can calculate how long a journey might take, or explain
aspects of a plot, relating the poorly drained fields of Grange Farm to their
location next to the River Am. We can also use maps to help re-imagine
events in the past, from the Borchester Mail Van Robbery of 1967, to the
gradual unfolding of events in the Titchener household in 2015–16. They
can help us to fix events, freeze time, and place and locate the stories that

emerge in *The Archers*. However, regarding maps as tools that simply depict the world greatly over-simplifies the social roles that they play (Wood 2010).

Mapping is also deployed in various attempts to relate the fictional Ambridge and Borsetshire to a 'real' placing of the village. Clearly these associations reflect a complex web of links, and most people accept that the programme might be loosely associated with the Evesham area and the village of Inkberrow on the Worcestershire–Warwickshire border. Mapping can, however, be enrolled in these debates to 'reify' possibly spurious claims. An animated gif file on a website with a fictional map morphing into a Google map of the real can be deployed to make the case for a link between Ambridge and the village of Hornton in Oxfordshire all the more plausible. We are somehow more likely to believe claims if they are mapped out.

Mapping also sells. Printing a map onto a piece of merchandise is part of a branding for real places and fulfils the same role for commercial publishers and the BBC in relation to Ambridge. Jigsaws, mugs, tea towels and quilts that incorporate mappings of Ambridge have been produced. Maps of the village can be downloaded as wallpaper for your website, purchased as a separate published item or sent to your friends as an ecard. So the map persuades as well as depicting places (Muehlenhaus 2013).

This selling of the place also entails an imitation of real world through the making of completely fictional historical mapping of Ambridge. As part of the spin-off literature, the 1981 publication of Jennifer Aldridge's and John Tregorran's [*sic*] *Ambridge: An English Village through the Ages* included spoof John Speed maps of Borsetshire, and mapping of the deserted medieval village under excavation at Grange Farm. This fake village history used fake mapping to make it more like real village histories.

This blurring of the real and the imaginary reached a climax with the 2015 floods. The BBC website charted the ongoing storyline of the floods in the village. A weather report emulated BBC website forecasting. A media map featured a concentric circle centred on the village. Smaller scale mapping highlighted sites along the River Am impacted by the event. Mapping served as functional glue to help explain events, but also made the floods more real, accompanying the spoken stories of the events and persuading readers (see Figure 15). Critical media coverage about this blurring may

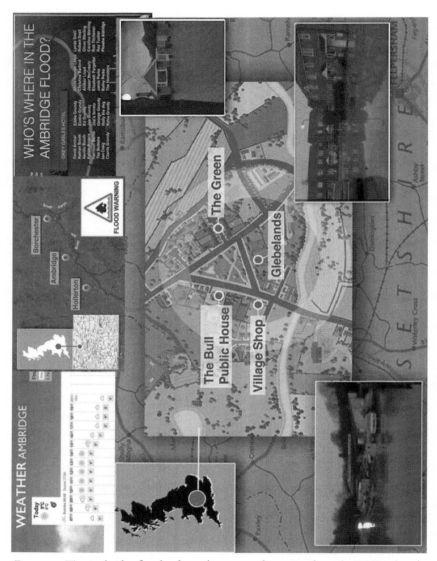

Figure 15: The Ambridge floods of 2015 (montage of mapping from the BBC website).

well have deterred a similar focus on real world stories since. It is interesting that the controversy over Route B and the Save Am Vale Campaign of the last two years has been almost completely unmapped.

It is not only publishers and the BBC who have used mapping to explore the relationship between the real and imaginary landscapes. Fans also take part in these debates, taking the landscape of Ambridge and extrapolating using their own imaginations, adding to the fantasy with maps of the range of a fictional transmitter on Hassett Hills and the impact of Beeching closures on the railway network of Borsetshire. We can all re-use web-served and published maps nowadays for our own purposes.

Missing from Ambridge ...

Shifts towards a focus on the wider social roles played by mapping have also encouraged us to examine what is not on maps. In Ambridge some things are strikingly absent. Cartography of the village does not seem to have to keep up with events. There is no legally defined obligation to ground the fantasy in the way in which Ordnance Survey is obligated to maintain a current coverage of the real world. The mega dairy episodes are quite hard to place, because Berrow Farm is absent on the maps. No attempt so far seemed to have been made to chart the detail of Routes A, B and C for the bypass story. Scales of depiction also limit what can be mapped. The internal layout of houses has not been included yet in the way that rightmove.co.uk or other websites incorporate house plans. But with characters forgetting rooms in their homes, such as Ruth Archer mislaying a bedroom for her mother to stay in (see Jo Moriarty's chapter in this volume), this might prove problematic. Powerful interests are strikingly off the map: thematic maps of poverty in the village or of landownership have not been published. Mapping tends to reinforce the image of a pastoral idyll, immune from the pressures of global capital. Emotions and feelings are very much off the Ambridge map as well. Conflict is rarely mapped out. Maps simply show what is where and focus on real tangible things.

Data can be layered to help readers explore patterns, instead of presenting them with interpretations from a publisher. Such facilities have to
date not been implemented in relation to Ambridge. Nor has there been
very much use of the medium to analyse storylines. We might speculate
that Lakey Hill plays a particular role in romantic trysts, or as a place for
evoking a sense of place. We might speculate that the true centre of the
village in terms of frequency of storylines remains Brookfield, but that
detail is absent in maps, despite a rich potential for maps as a medium to
tell particular stories (Caquard 2013). Instead published maps of Ambridge
mostly work as traditional topographic frameworks. It is interesting that
the BBC chose to take down its interactive map of the village from the
web site in 2010, perhaps to increase the mystery. Maybe there are some
things that people do not wish to be mapped.

Conclusions

My argument in this chapter has been that people can use the mapping of
imaginary places like Ambridge in a number of different ways. The ground-
ing, fixing and placing of events is certainly something that these maps
do. But to limit mapping to this kind of role, serving as a type of spatial
index to events, is to underestimate the power of the medium. Maps sell
places. They also help us to tell stories. They link the real to the imagined.
The sheep on Lakey Hill depicted on the map frontispiece to William
Smethurst's (1980) *The Archers: The First Thirty Years* (see Figure 16)
tell us as much about the map as the symbols depicting buildings on
Smethurst's thirty-five-year-old map. They set the tone of the image.
    I have suggested instead of just looking at maps of Ambridge we should
think about how they might be deployed and of the new possibilities they
might bring into play. These maps are partial records of the place, just as
flawed as a Google map on a mobile device directing a smartphone user
to a restaurant that reflects browsing history. Mapping Ambridge is also
personal and political. The maps of the village construct Ambridge, as
well as depicting the place. Just like maps of real places maps of fantasy
landscapes do more than just locate events. And these maps paradoxically

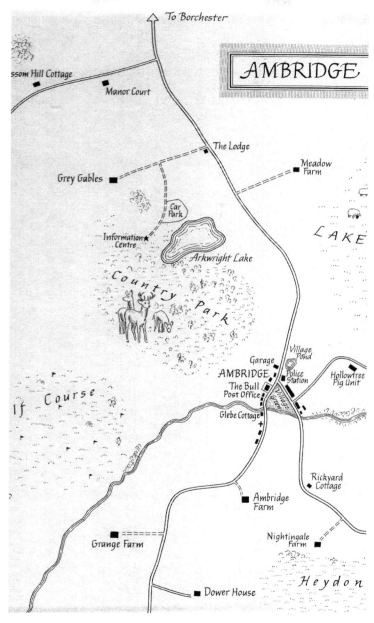

Figure 16: The sheep on Lakey Hill (extract from map frontispiece to William Smethurst's *The Archers: The First Thirty Years* (London: Eyre Methuen, 1980).

become all the more important precisely because of the imaginary nature of the village. They become part of the fantasy of listening. Together with other media they come together to make a sense of Ambridge. They make the place all the more real, whilst preserving our capacity to imagine.

References

Balfe, M. (2004). 'Incredible Geographies? Orientalism and Genre Fantasy', *Social & Cultural Geography* 5.1: 75–90.

Caquard, S. (2013). 'Cartography I: Mapping Narrative Cartography', *Progress in Human Geography* 37.1: 135–44.

Dodge, M., R. Kitchin, and C. Perkins (eds) (2009). *Rethinking Maps: New Frontiers in Cartographic Theory*. London: Routledge.

Dykes, J., A. M. MacEachren and M. J. Kraak (2005). *Exploring Geovisualization*. New York: Elsevier.

Edney, M. H. (1993). 'Cartography without Progress: Reinterpreting the Nature and Historical Development of Mapmaking', *Cartographica: The International Journal for Geographic Information and Geovisualization* 30.2–3: 54–68.

Harmon, K. A. (2004). *You Are Here: Personal Geographies and Other Maps of the Imagination*. New York: Princeton Architectural Press.

Muehlenhaus, I. (2013). 'The Design and Composition of Persuasive Maps', *Cartography and Geographic Information Science* 40.5: 401–14.

Perkins, C. (2007). 'Mapping'. In R. Huggett, I. Douglas and C. Perkins (eds), *Companion Encyclopaedia of Geography*. London: Routledge: 553–70.

Wood, D. (2010). *Rethinking the Power of Maps*. New York: Guilford Press.

Review by Jennifer Aldridge, Home Farm, Ambridge

Email
From: Jennifer.Aldridge@homefarm.com
To: Robert.Snell@llamasrus.com

Dear Robert

Just read Chris's chapter about the mapping of Ambridge and it reminded me of the work I did over thirty years ago with my dear friend John – such a shame we lost touch. What a loss. I really miss him.

Anyway – I didn't really like Chris's jibes about things being left off the map – it almost reads like a conspiracy. But I really liked his idea that maps can sell a place – why don't we put Ambridge on the map again Robert? I saw this website about the Parish Maps Project (https://www.commonground.org.uk/parish-maps) and all the wonderful celebration of creative energy mapped out by villages across the country. I can't believe we failed to make one when the project was launched all those years ago. There's so much going on in Ambridge.

Wouldn't it be a great opportunity to bring people together by making a parish map of the village? And by using all your web expertise to make it interactive, so that everyone everywhere can find out about our history, our artistic projects, our small businesses and the energy around Ambridge? The Save Am Vale victory shows our community spirit – the map could get even more people involved but also showing how important it is to preserve everything we stand for. I'm sure Lynda and Susan would love to get involved. Even Brian! He seems to love playing with that GPS-driven crop management system that Adam is now using. Everyone seems to love maps. We could use the web to make it work and fill in the gap that the BBC left when they took down our village mapping!

What a great opportunity and way to bring everyone together. Let me know what you think.

Best wishes
Jennifer

PETER MATTHEWS

Lynda Snell, Class Warrior: Social Class and Community Activism in Rural Borsetshire

New residents always cause upset in rural Borsetshire. Most recently we have: Rob Titchener (the less said about him the better); PC Harrison Burns causing a stir among the women; and Justin Elliott of Damara Capital, the mastermind behind Route B, the road that almost saw the Archers leaving Bridge Farm, and scourge of Lynda Snell and the 'Boudicca of Borsetshire' Jennifer Aldridge, as they fought to save the Am Vale. Residents of Ambridge know that Lynda Snell is a relative newcomer herself, compared to the centuries of history of the Archer and Grundy clans. She and her husband Robert recently commemorated their thirty years in the village with the building of a shepherd's hut. As such, Lynda and Robert represent a key pattern that has marked the British countryside in the post-war years – the in-migration of commuters and retirees into more rural locations from the suburbs of larger towns and cities. There is an extensive literature on 'rural gentrification' and the impact of in-movers such as the Snells. This chapter rather concentrates on the impact of these in-movers on what we might term the civic and associational life of the Ambridge: the Parish Council, the annual Christmas shows and all the collective actions that helped shape the place and community.

Community Activism as Classed Practice

In a review of the literature and research Matthews and Hastings (2013) found strong evidence that middle-class people are more civically active, and that they are more likely to be successful in their activities. They found that there are four key ways in which middle-class people achieve this impact. First, 'I'll join the parish council': middle-class people are more likely to join groups and join groups that matter, that policy-makers listen to, such as parish councils, school governing boards and amenity associations. Second, 'I'll email my councillor and complain': middle-class people, or people with higher household incomes or socio-economic status, complain more than non-middle-class people. There is also evidence of a positive feedback loop: these people complain, get a positive response, and then have learnt how to manage the system so complain more in future. Third, 'I'll just phone my friend, the doctor': most professionals are middle class, so middle-class people are likely to have them in their social networks. Furthermore, they also use the same language and share other social mores which make communication more effective. Fourth, 'I'll vote for them': from the early 1980s there has been successive research showing that party manifestos prioritize the needs of middle-class voters, issues such as healthcare and education. Matthews and Hastings (ibid.) also found evidence that service providers or developers (such as house builders) would adjust their strategies and delivery to anticipate an imagined vociferous middle class.

Lynda Snell is Middle Class

How does Lynda Snell embody middle-class behaviours? When Lynda moved to Ambridge, one of her first activities, as she recounts herself, was to join the parish council (Snell 1997). This is a classic example of the ways in which middle-class people rapidly establish their social capital when they move to a new location. As Bagnall et al. (2003) found in their research in semi-rural and suburban Cheshire, joining groups – in their case the local parent–teachers association – is a key way of new residents settling in to new social networks and getting to know people like themselves. These groups are dominated by middle-class people like themselves so it is a quick and easy way to make friendships and develop social networks. Thus, while the Ambridge Parish Council may have been more diverse than Lynda might have been expecting, she quickly ascended to become chair, a position of some importance within local social networks.

In recent years, Lynda has extended this by creating new groups – most recently, Save the Am Vale Environment, or SAVE, the campaign against

Route B. Whereas much of her campaigning on local developments has been on an individual basis, this time Lynda, and the rest of the villagers, realized a group response was necessary. Like the residents discussed in the research by Abram et al. (1996) the residents of Ambridge had learnt to engage early in the processes. They were not waiting for Route B to be announced, but were actively arguing why Route B should not be considered at all. But just like the wind farm developers researched by Walker et al. (2010), Damara Capital and the other sponsors of Route B had their arguments against the campaigners ready – particularly in terms of the number of jobs it would create, a key way to gain support for controversial developments (Matthews et al. 2015).

As mentioned, Lynda also likes complaining herself against specific issues – she was vociferous in her objection to the mega dairy developed by Borchester Land. This was the latest in a series of planning complaints. Early on in her life in Ambridge she got involved with the Borsetshire Environment Trust to get a hedge designated as a Site of Special Scientific Interest subject to environmental protection, to prevent the Grundy family from removing it. Lynda also lodged an objection to Susan Carter's neo-Georgian front door in the sensitive rural setting of Ambridge (Snell 1997). When Lynda does complain, she demonstrates the adeptness of a typical middle-class person in using the right language and correct technical terms, for example when she recently campaigned against the mega-diary on public health grounds following the outbreak of Botulism.

Lynda's ability to deploy her social capital – her links to people like herself – invariably come in useful when she turns her hand to the annual Christmas show, the highlight of the cultural calendar in Ambridge. Invariably, at the last minute a key cast member will drop out, much to Lynda's dismay. However, with her links into the local amateur dramatics scene Lynda quickly finds a suitable replacement to play the role. This ability to connect to the right people has also come in useful during Lynda's Route B campaign. Through her friendship with David Archer she was able to access the environmental consultants that could formulate the environmental arguments against Route B, networks that most people simply do not have.

Lynda Snell as Place-maker

In all these ways Lynda Snell recreates the sort of middle-class behaviour we would expect from the research. What is more important, though, is the way in which these behaviours are place-making and place-shaping. When people such as Robert and Lynda Snell move to somewhere like Ambridge they, in the terminology of Savage (2010), *electively belong*. Whereas for the Grundy family, Ambridge is a place of social and familial connections, a comfort of what Allen (2008) refers to as 'we-being', for the Snells it is a wider part of their identity, how they portray themselves to others.

A key way Lynda achieves this is through her use of her cultural capital – the social mores and taste she has (Bourdieu 1986). Lynda articulated this class positioning in relation to Susan Carter: 'I know that Susan regards me as something of a role-model – ever since the day I offered her a glass of sherry'. Moreover, Lynda could not forego the opportunity to take part in Anthony Gormley's (2009) *One and Other* fourth-plinth art work in Trafalgar Square, a key way to demonstrate she was a woman of cultural sophistication.

In having elective belonging, middle-class people like the Snells are buying into a specific way of life and identity – in this case the life of a rural idyll like Ambridge. Therefore, if this investment in money and emotion is threatened, they respond by protecting that sense of belonging (Watt 2009). As Watt found, such people deploy exactly the same tactics as Lynda Snell: using their social networks to access specialist help such as lawyers to make a successful argument to protect what they have electively, or in Watt's case, selectively, chosen to belong too.

As well as this activist sensibility, Lynda also displays more subtle ways in which she deploys her cultural capital to make Ambridge the way she has always imagined it to be. We have already mentioned her discontent with Susan Carter choosing a mock-Georgian front door, but in their thirtieth year in Ambridge, Lynda decided to celebrate by commissioning a shepherd's hut for the garden of Ambridge Hall. The response of most residents of the Am Vale to this news was to quickly search for what a shepherd's hut actually was. While these little caravans used to have widespread use in the countryside, modern farming methods mean they are now a rarity, more commonly seen in gardens as an ornamental feature. Yet they evoke a rural idyll – of the hard-pressed shepherd, tending the flock of a cool spring evening. As she commented on 15 April 2016, the hut is 'a homage to a bygone time [... it] represents a rural idyll'. This idyll has long since passed in Ambridge, with the mega-dairy and the threat of Route B changing the countryside forever: in buying her shepherd's hut, Lynda is pushing-back against this progress.

Lynda Snell as Class Warrior

The representations of Lynda Snell's classed practice so far have been relatively benign. Although we have demonstrated that she is very middle class and behaves in ways that are demonstrably middle class based on existing evidence, this is either to the benefit of Ambridge, or in a model of an almost patrician concern for the environment. However, when Bourdieu (1986) theorized about social and cultural capital he argued that it was also deployed in a way that was class-interested – the successful use of capital means more capital (economic, social or cultural) is accumulated and class inequalities further entrenched.

We can see the critical outcome of this in terms of the impact on the delivery of housing in rural areas. The trend of more affluent incomers, such as the Snells, moving into rural villages has led to a widely known problem with house-price inflation and low housing supply that puts housing out of reach for people in low-paid agricultural or tourist jobs in the countryside. A key way of delivering new affordable housing is through 'exceptions' housing (Yarwood 2002). This means that, where a local plan would stop any new housing development in a village to protect its character, an exception is made where it is affordable housing to buy or rent from a housing association designated through a Section 106 planning agreement.

These have become a common tool in the English planning system. A key challenge has been though, that while many people such as the Snells would welcome new affordable housing for local families such as Ed and

Emma Grundy, housing law means such housing has to be made available to everyone on the housing list at Borchester District Council. While the Snells, Aldridges and Archers would welcome the Grundys as neighbours, they might be less welcoming of a Tucker or Horrobin.

As discussed earlier, middle-class activists are very good at learning about complex policy mechanisms, such as planning systems (Abram et al. 1996). Many realized this issue with 'exceptions' housing and forced developing housing associations to add unenforceable 'locality' clauses to the new houses (Yarwood 2002). This constant action by middle-class parish councillors was clearly driven by snobbery of having to live next to lower-class people who were not like them, as clearly shown by this shocking quote from Sturzaker's study (2010) of rural housing supply: 'In order to keep riff-raff from [nearby city] out of the community you need this s106 Agreement [planning policy]' (1014). Indeed, Sturzaker's work on the former planning system in England of Regional Spatial Strategies demonstrated that regions with many villages, like Ambridge, saw the biggest reductions in proposed housing numbers over the course of plan preparation, most likely due to middle-class opposition.

So, such activity is not benign; Lynda Snell is not the new patrician Lady of the Manor in a bucolic countryside. If Lynda's opposition to Route B and the associated economic development is successful, then Edward and Emma Grundy, and when they grow up George and Keira, might not have access to good-quality, semi-skilled, secure employment locally. The pressure to reduce the volume of new houses being built and the impact of incomers and non-resident landlords such as Hazel Woolley changing their housing to suit a more middle class-market all create structural reasons for the homelessness of families like Clarrie, Eddie and Joe Grundy.

There is a class war in Ambridge and Lynda Snell is a class warrior. The battle of tastes and class position is wrought through small incidents such as Lynda trying to persuade Bert Fry not to overshadow the opening of her *Resurgam* garden with his own garden opening in memory to his late vociferous wife Freda. The class war manifests itself in the ongoing class-interested actions of people such as Lynda, shaping the countryside to their idealized bucolic image.

References

Abram, S., J. Murdoch and T. Marsden (1996). 'The Social Construction of "Middle England": The Politics of Participation in Forward Planning', *Journal of Rural Studies* 12.4: 353–64.

Allen, C. (2008). *Housing Market Renewal and Social Class*. Abingdon: Routledge.

Bagnall, G., B. Longhurst and M. Savage (2003). 'Children, Belonging and Social Capital: The PTA and Middle Class Narratives of Social Involvement in the North-West of England', *Sociological Research Online* 8.4.

Bourdieu, P. (1986). *The Forms of Capital: Handbook of Theory and Research for the Sociology of Education*, ed. J. G. Richardson. New York: Greenwood: 241–58.

Ellis, G. (2004). 'Discourses of Objection: Towards an Understanding of Third-Party Rights in Planning', *Environment and Planning A* 36.9: 1549–70.

Matthews, P., G. Bramley and A. Hastings (2015). 'Homo Economicus in a Big Society: Understanding Middle-Class Activism and NIMBYism towards New Housing Developments', *Housing, Theory and Society* 32.1: 54–72.

Matthews, P., and A. Hastings (2013). 'Middle-Class Political Activism and Middle-Class Advantage in Relation to Public Services: A Realist Synthesis of the Evidence Base', *Social Policy & Administration* 47.1: 72–92.

Putnam, R. (2000). *Bowling Alone: The Collapse and Revival of American Community*. New York: Touchstone.

Savage, M. (2010). 'Class and Elective Belonging', *Housing, Theory and Society* 27.2: 115–36.

Snell, L. (1997). *Heritage of Ambridge*. London: Virgin Books.

Sturzaker, J. (2010). 'The Exercise of Power to Limit the Development of New Housing in the English Countryside', *Environment and Planning A* 42.4: 1001–16.

Walker, G., N. Cass, K. Burningham and J. Barnett (2010). 'Renewable Energy and Sociotechnical Change: Imagined Subjectivities of "the Public" and their Implications', *Environment and Planning A* 42.4: 931–47.

Watt, P. (2009). 'Living in an Oasis: Middle-Class Disaffiliation and Selective Belonging in an English Suburb', *Environment and Planning A* 41.12: 2874–92.

Yarwood, R. (2002). 'Parish Councils, Partnership and Governance: The Development of "Exceptions" Housing in the Malvern Hills District, England', *Journal of Rural Studies* 18.3: 275–91.

Review by Lynda Snell, Ambridge Hall, Ambridge, Borsetshire

Middle-class warrior, *me*?! Acting in my own self-interest? I'll have this jumped-up envy-driven author trying to pass off as an intellectual know that everything I do is in the interests of all residents of Ambridge. How can they discount my years of work for the parish council? Where would the village shop be, if it wasn't for me gathering the troops together to get it running? And the SAVE campaign is definitely not in my interest! The hours I spend on the thankless task, for a road that will actually make it easier for me to pop to Underwood's in Borchester. And I could go and visit little Mungo so much more easily with the new road! The author really must read Ellis (2004) who makes it quite clear that objectors to developments are only doing so because they have the wider interests of the environment at heart. And this nonsense about my social and cultural capital. I *made* Susan the woman she is today! She looks up to me. She's transformed into a lively member of the community. The author should pay much more attention to Robert Putnam (2000) – the social capital I develop makes the village come alive! It's why we've all clubbed together to repair the village hall; it's why we can all trust that there will be a happy and willing volunteer at the village shop.

JO MORIARTY

The Death of Heather Pritchard: An Everyday Story of Inadequate Social Care

The death of Ruth Archer's mother, Heather Pritchard, in a motorway cafe car park on the M1 on 28 September 2015 made a dramatic culmination to her reluctant decision to move to Brookfield. Older Ambridge residents, such as Joe Grundy (born in 1921) and Peggy Archer (born in 1924), generally conform to the stereotype of the 'rural idyll' in which ageing is largely a process of minor adjustment. Heather perhaps offers a more typical example in which increasing frailty leads to a need for more social care support. Social care is not a new topic in The Archers. *It was extensively covered in the decade 2004–2014 through the much-praised storyline of Jack Woolley's dementia. As he gradually needed more assistance, his wife Peggy recruited a number of care workers to help her look after Jack in their home, The Lodge. Eventually, he moved to The Laurels, a nursing home, in 2009 where he died in 2014 (Davies 2014). The over representation of migrant workers in the social care workforce (Hussein et al. 2011) was mirrored through the character of Elona Makepeace, who was born in Albania. This chapter uses the death of Heather Pritchard to discuss aspects of rural social care, theories about social networks and ageing in place, and the increasing number of distance carers (family members providing unpaid care at a distance) in the United Kingdom. The contrast between the potential support that could have been offered to Heather and Ruth and their actual experiences is almost as dramatic as Heather's death. Arguably, however, it better exemplifies the considerable barriers that confront many older people in finding the sort of care that they want and need.*

Social Networks and Ageing

The concept of social networks is fundamental to gerontology (the study of the social, psychological, cognitive and biological aspects of ageing). It encompasses the different types and frequency of interpersonal contacts that people have and which provide them with access to social, emotional and practical support (Gray 2009; Litwin and Stoeckel 2013). Networks evolve during people's lives, through experiences such as school, employ-ment, marriage, parenthood and retirement – hence the phrase 'convoy model' used to describe social support over the lifetime (Antonucci and Akiyama 1987).

In old age, bereavement and illness often lead to a reduction in social networks. This may be accompanied by a transition from using so-called 'informal', sources of support from a range of family and friends, towards reliance upon unpaid care from a family member, usually a spouse or adult child, and paid care (Chappell and Blandford 1991; Davey et al. 2005). Different types of network are associated with different levels of service utilization, so somebody with a dense network of local family and friends is likely to need less 'formal' support than a person with a more restricted social network (Wenger and Tucker 2002).

Heather Pritchard and Jill Archer, the mothers of Ruth and David Archer respectively, were both widows and shared a friendly rivalry, often accompanied by undertones about their contrasting positions. Heather chose to stay in Prudhoe following the death of her husband Solly in 2002. Although Jill temporarily lived on her own in Glebe Cottage after Phil died in 2010, she eventually moved back to Brookfield in 2014, following a burglary. Another contrast between Heather and Jill was that Ruth was Heather's only child and lived at a distance. Jill has four children who all live nearby.

Crucially, if a person needs help with activities such as washing, going to the lavatory or eating, this is almost always provided by family members or, in their absence, by paid workers. It is rarely provided by neighbours or volunteers (Alcock and May 2014). Although Heather was a sociable woman with a capacity for friendship – she shared Phil's liking for musi-cals and they went to several concerts together (much to Jill's irritation) (Toye and Farrington 2013), her social networks were much less extensive.

Despite the comparative cheapness of options that would have helped substitute for some of these gaps, such as an alarm system or movement sensors that would alert people to the fact she had fallen, Heather was very reliant upon one neighbour and extended visits from Ruth in the last few months of her life. Eventually, this level of support proved to be insufficient, leading to her reluctant decision to move to Brookfield and Jill's temporary displacement to Lower Loxley.

Social Care: What It Is and Who Pays For It

> Social care covers a wide range of services, both private and public, and
> can include anything from help getting out of bed and washing, through
> to care homes and drop-in centres.
>
> — Age UK, 2016

Unlike care provided through the National Health Service, access to publicly funded social care is means tested and arranged through local councils.
Expenditure on social care has not kept pace with increases in numbers of
older people and people with disabilities. Allowing for inflation, the amount
that local councils in England spend on social care is actually 10 per cent
less than in 2009 (Humphries and Appleby 2015). They have tried to cope
with this shortfall by raising the criteria by which people become eligible
for local authority funded social care so that only those with the highest
needs for support qualify for assistance. This has led to a reduction of
26 per cent in the number of people receiving social care arranged by their
local authority (Fernandez et al. 2013). Pressure has also been placed on
providers to reduce costs when bidding for local authority contracts, creating large increases in the number of social care workers employed on zero-
hours contracts and paid at little more than the national minimum wage
(Moriarty 2015). Indeed, 9–13 per cent of home care workers are estimated
to receive even less than the national minimum wage, mainly because they
are not paid for travelling time between appointments (Gardiner 2015).

We know from Heather's will that she owned a house and had a life
insurance policy, each worth £250,000. This meant that, like Jack Woolley,
her assets were well in excess of the current capital and savings limits above
which people have to pay for all of their social care until the point at which
their assets become so depleted that they become eligible for publicly
funded care. At the time of writing, this limit is £23,250 in England (NHS
Choices 2015). A 'cap' of £72,000 on lifetime care costs was to be introduced in April 2016 but has been delayed until 2020. The cap will help
people who fund their care over a number of years, such as Jack Woolley,
but not those such as Heather who need care over a comparatively short
period. Arrangements are slightly different in Scotland, Wales and Northern

Ireland but it probably would not have been a good idea for Heather to have moved to another country in the United Kingdom simply to avoid care costs without taking legal advice first.

The jargon used to describe people in Heather's position is 'self-funders'. It is estimated that 43 per cent of older and physically disabled adult residents of independent care homes fund the entire cost of their care (Humphries 2013). However, the proportion in the North East is only 36 per cent, a smaller proportion than in any other part of England (Baxter and Glendinning 2014). We must assume that Heather's inclusion in this group is largely down to her husband's having been a 'reasonably successful toilet paper manufacturer' (Smith 2015).

Another 14 per cent of care home residents 'top up' local authority funding with some additional private spending (Humphries 2013), usually paid by other family members but sometimes by charitable trusts, especially those supporting people who have worked in a particular trade or occupation or their families. These sums are important. Many care homes will not accept residents whose care is wholly paid by the local council because they consider that the amounts offered are insufficient. Being able to afford a 'top up' fee enables people to have a greater choice over the care home in which they live and perhaps also cover 'extras', such as activities and outings. In what seems to be yet another unfair comparison between the Pritchard and Archer families, there does not appear to be a charitable organization helping with top up fees for toilet paper manufacturers who have fallen on hard times but the Royal Agricultural Benevolent Institution (RABI) offers support with top up fees for people from a farming background and even runs two care homes of its own.

Joe, Heather and the Care Act 2014

The Care Act 2014 marked a major overhaul of social care legislation. It placed a new duty on local authorities to ensure that all residents, whatever their funding arrangements, could get the information and advice they needed to make good decisions about their care and support. The charity Independent Age (Qa Research 2016) undertook a series of 'mystery shopper' calls in which older people called up local council advice lines across the country with a series of hypothetical questions about the help they could expect. Based on this information, Independent Age concluded that most councils were only meeting the 'legal minimum' (4).

One of the difficulties for those arranging social care is that people often only seek help once a crisis has occurred. Although Joe Grundy often says he does not want to live in a care home, he seems unaware of what his options really are. When Hazel Woolley ended the Grundys' tenancy of Keeper's Cottage, Joe, Clarrie and Eddie were forced to look for somewhere else to live. Before Oliver and Caroline Sterling offered them the temporary tenancy of Grange Farm (which the Grundys had farmed until their eviction), it appeared that Joe might have to temporarily live in a hostel. As well as highlighting the lack of affordable housing in rural areas (Rural Housing Policy Review 2015), this also drew attention to limitations in the performance of Borsetshire Adult Social Care. They seem to have made no attempt to explain to Joe what choices were available or to present him with any alternatives. Of even greater concern is that given Joe's age (currently ninety-four, as he reminds everyone), they do not seem to have assessed what he could do unaided and whether he needed any additional support. Of course, this would have been a difficult task. Joe's difficulties seem very selective. While he seems unable to help Clarrie with any household tasks, he can certainly get to the orchard with Jim Lloyd to test the cider.

As mentioned earlier, Heather's financial situation meant that she would not have been eligible for any support from her local council. However, as the number of visits that Ruth needed to make to visit Heather in Northumberland increased and it became clear that Heather was unable to live alone independently but did not wish to move to a care home, the decision that Heather should move down to Brookfield was presented as the only option. Alternatives such as extra care housing, assistive technology, and adapted housing did not seem to have been discussed. In the same way, Ruth's statutory entitlement under the Care Act 2014 to have her needs as a carer assessed does not seem to have been considered.

'Ageing in Place'

Both Heather and Joe expressed a preference not to move into a care home. The phrase that is often used to describe people's preference to remain in their own homes, or at least their own neighbourhoods, is 'ageing in place' (Wiles et al. 2012). Despite the availability of alternatives such as telecare and housing adaptations, or even extra care housing where people retain their own 'front door' but can access help from care workers to help them remain living independently, Heather does not seem to have been offered these potential solutions.

It has always cost more to provide services such as home care in rural settings because of the additional travel time need for workers to travel between visits (United Kingdom Home Care Association 2015). The provision of extra care housing is also less frequent (Connors et al. 2013b) although there is at least one extra care housing provider in Prudhoe. There were other limitations in the support Heather appeared to receive – most notably in terms information about advance care planning and her rights under the Mental Capacity Act 2005, best illustrated when Heather absconded from the care home in which she had been living temporarily to go home. Little attempt seems to have been made to explain this situation to Ruth and to provide support for her as a distance carer and, subsequently as a bereaved person.

Discussion

Proportionally, more older people live in rural areas than large towns and cities (Connors et al. 2013a). Rising rural house prices have created increased geographical mobility, as illustrated by Emma and Ed's difficulty in finding a house they can afford. There seems little evidence that Borsetshire Council is making many attempts to plan for these changes and to fulfil their obligations under the Care Act 2014 to ensure that residents have access to a range of good quality social care services. The increase in the number of older people living in rural areas and the lack of social care services means that much will depend on family carers, such as Ruth. This suggests that Heather's situation – if not her mode of death – will be increasingly common.

References

Age UK (2016). *Social Care and Support – All You Need To Know* <http://www.ageuk. org.uk/home-and-care/help-at-home/social-care---all-you-need-to-know/> accessed 28 June 2016.

Alcock, P., and M. May (2014). *Social Policy in Britain*. Basingstoke: Palgrave Macmillan.

Antonucci, T., and H. Akiyama (1987). 'Gender and Social Support Networks in Later Life', *Journal of Gerontology* 42: 519–27.

Baxter, K., and C. Glendinning (2014). *People Who Fund Their Own Social Care.* London: NIHR School for Social Care.

Chappell, N., and A. Blandford (1991). 'Informal and Formal Care: Exploring the Complementarity', *Ageing and Society* 11: 299–317.

Connors, C., M. Kenrick and A. Bloch (2013a). *2013 Rural Ageing Research Summary Report of Findings.* London: TNS BRMB & International Longevity Centre (ILC).

Connors, C., M. Kenrick and A. Bloch (2013b). *Impact of an Ageing Population on Service Design and Delivery in Rural Areas. Qualitative Research.* London: Department for Environment Food and Rural Affairs.

Davey, A., E. E. Femia, S. H. Zarit, D. G. Shea, G. Sundström, S. Berg, M. A. Smyer and J. Savla (2005). 'Life on the Edge: Patterns of Formal and Informal Help to Older Adults in the United States and Sweden', *Journals of Gerontology Series B: Psychological Sciences and Social Sciences* 60: S281–S288.

Davies, K. (2014). 'Jack Woolley 1919 to 2014', *The Archers Blog* <http://www.bbc. co.uk/blogs/thearchers/entries/949bc08e-bf04-38c5-90d0-b501e4015a59> accessed 28 June 2016.

Fernandez, J. L., T. Snell and G. Wistow (2013). *Changes in the Patterns of Social Care Provision in England: 2005/6 to 2012/13. PSSRU Discussion Paper 2867.* Canterbury: Personal Social Services Research Unit.

Gardiner, L. (2015). *The Scale of Minimum Wage Underpayment in Social Care*. London: Resolution Foundation.

Gray, A. (2009). 'The Social Capital of Older People', *Ageing & Society* 29: 5–31.

Humphries, R. (2013). *Paying for Social Care: Deyond Dilnot*. London: King's Fund.

Humphries, R., and J. Appleby (2015). 'Social Care: A Future We Don't Yet Know', *King's Fund Blog* <http://www.kingsfund.org.uk/blog/2015/11/social-care-future> accessed 28 June 2016.

Hussein, S., M. Stevens and J. Manthorpe (2011). 'What drives the recruitment of Migrant Workers to Work in Social Care in England?', *Social Policy and Society* 10: 285–98.

Litwin, H., and K. J. Stoeckel (2013). 'Social Networks and Subjective Wellbeing Among Older Europeans: Does Age Make a Difference?', *Ageing & Society* 33: 1263–81.

Moriarty, J. (2015). 'Chapter Four Commentary: The Adult Social Care Workforce in England'. In D. Walden (ed.), *Reimagining Adult Social Care Evidence Review*. Dartington: Research in Practice for Adults.

NHS Choices (2015). *Funding Care* <http://www.nhs.uk/Conditions/social-care-and-support-guide/Pages/funding-care.aspx> accessed 28 June 2016.

Qa Research (2016). *Information and Advice Since the Care Act: How Are Councils Performing?* London: Independent Age.

Royal Agricultural Benevolent Institution (2016). *Residential Care* <http://rabi.org.uk/need-help/residential-care/> accessed 28 June 2016.

Rural Housing Policy Review (2015). *Affordable Housing: A Fair Deal for Rural Communities. Report of the Rural Housing Policy Review*. Web-based publication.

Smith, A. (2015). 'Heather Pritchard: Mistress of Marmalade and Beloved Mum of Ruth', *The Archers Blog* <http://www.bbc.co.uk/blogs/thearchers/entries/14fc6015-cec3-4333-8b3b-5d7583a46ac2> accessed 28 June 2016.

Toye, J., and K. Farrington (2013). *The Ambridge Chronicles: Moments that Made the Nation's Favourite Radio Drama*. London: BBC Books.

United Kingdom Home Care Association (2015). *The Home Care Deficit: A Report on the Funding of Older People's Homecare Across the United Kingdom*. London: United Kingdom Home Care Association.

Wenger, G. C., and I. Tucker (2002). 'Using Network Variation in Practice: Identification of Support Network Type', *Health and Social Care in the Community* 10: 28–35.

Wiles, J. L., A. Leibing, N. Guberman, J. Reeve and R. E. S. Allen (2012). 'The Meaning of "Aging in Place" to Older People', *The Gerontologist* 52: 357–66.

Review by Ruth Archer, Bridge Farm, Ambridge

When I read this, I immediately thought, 'Oh nooooo'. I know I am not supposed to say that anymore to avoid being the object of almost every comedian's jokes on Radio 4 but it was no joke for me and me mam. We thought there was no alternative but for David, Pip, Josh and Ben to move to Prudhoe or – once David had his vision – for me mam to come to Brookfield. Actually, I've been looking at other chapters in this book and I'm not too pleased that me and me mam's last few months were just a narrative prosthesis. OK, so I missed the great flood but it was no fun driving up and down to Prudhoe for months on end while listeners wondered if Route B meant that we would have to sell Brookfield. It's also true that no one bothered to talk about end-of-life plans with me mam. For all I know, she might have wanted to go quickly, even if it was in a service station car park. No wonder after all this that I felt I had to go to New Zealand. OK, so the scenery was better than the view from a bereavement charity's office would have been but it still would have been nice to have had someone say to me 'Ruth, how are you?' I suppose if I hadn't gone to New Zealand I wouldn't have learned about the new methods of dairy farming with a smaller herd but while me mam's death meant that I could afford my new Herefords, I still really miss her and wish that she had had some more choices about how to spend her last few months.

DEBORAH BOWMAN

From Dr Locke's Boundaries to Carol's Confession: On Medical Ethics in *The Archers*

The Archers has frequently engaged with medicine, but much less with medical ethics, despite the moral content of many of the storylines. This chapter discusses the different ways in which medical ethics have been presented (and sometimes overlooked) and explored in The Archers. *The period covered in the chapter dates from the point at which the author first became an avid* Archers *listener as an awkward teenager in the mid-1980s to the present day. The chapter considers the extent to which the ethical questions and responses of characters in* The Archers *reflect current discourse, standards and practice in medical ethics drawing on two principal storylines, namely: Dr Locke's personal and professional relationship with Shula; and Carol's confession to Jennifer regarding her husband's death. It is argued that medical ethics, as a subject inherently concerned with conflict and disagreement, is the stuff of rich drama. Moreover, in a programme in which medical stories have been a recurrent and powerful theme, the relative absence of medical ethics is a surprising oversight that has, on occasion, resulted in some curious outcomes.*

Whither Medical Ethics in *The Archers*?

Illness and its consequences have recurred as storylines in *The Archers*. Physical and mental ill health have been equally well explored with memorable moments ranging from Chris Carter's cleft lip to Ruth's breast cancer and from George Barford's depression to Jack Woolley's dementia. Indeed, it has been suggested (Stepney 2011) that Ambridge is a disproportionately risky place to live with incidences of serious accidents and suicide considerably more frequent than the national average.

The impact of these medical storylines has been considerable with some (Bolton 2000) even attributing their choice of medicine as a career and ongoing professional development to listening to the programme. The stories are well-researched and those engaged in working with the editorial team describe a thorough and enjoyable process of collaboration (Dover 1989). Occasionally, doctors have been part of the programme itself, for example, when Robert Winston, the fertility expert, made a cameo appearance as Hayley Tucker's consultant in 2007. Access to healthcare in Ambridge appears to be good. Stepney (2011) notes that Lizzie Pargetter was one of fewer than one hundred people to receive a life-saving implant in 2009. The surgeries that are most likely to be used by residents of Ambridge are located in Hollerton and Borchester (Toye 2009). However, there have been a number of doctors living in the village and Ambridge Hall was originally the doctor's home (Dillon 2003).

Given the extensive range of illness and trauma that have befallen those who live in Ambridge, it is surprising that medical ethics has not featured more prominently. Indeed, questions of medical ethics are not merely absent, but, it is suggested, often overlooked or misrepresented. This oversight was particularly significant in the case of Dr Richard Locke.

Dr Richard Locke and the Problem of Boundaries

Richard Locke first arrived in Ambridge in 1992. His early years in Ambridge were relatively uneventful. Although, it is noteworthy that he was much involved in supporting Shula after the death of her husband, Mark, in 1994, continuing to give her fertility injections and confirming her pregnancy the week after she became a widow. In 1998 Shula was increasingly concerned about her son, Daniel, who was also registered as Richard Locke's patient. Richard, to the chagrin of Alistair whom Shula had been dating, became Shula's principal source of support. Soon, the relationship between Richard Locke and Shula was romantic and culminated in Shula being asked by Richard to consider making a future with him.

The relationship between Shula and Richard Locke is an exemplar of boundary crossing (Gutheil and Gabbard 1993). The concept of boundaries has been variously described but all interpretations commonly encapsulate the notion of the limits that exist (physical, behavioural and emotional) to ensure a safe and effective therapeutic or working relationship. Boundaries are the fence within which a secure, clearly delineated professional space is created and maintained thereby defining a professional relationship or duty of care between a patient and doctor. They recognize that the relationship is unique. Boundaries matter because of the stubbornly constant power that resides in healthcare professionals' daily work. For, however much knowledge is accessible, and shared rather than rarefied, there is an unavoidable power imbalance. The patient has a problem and needs the clinician's advice, opinion or skills. The patient is dependent in a way that the clinician is not in the encounter. The trick then is not to seek to eliminate power, but to recognize it as inevitable and facilitate mutual trust and respect. Boundaries provide a framework within which all clinicians should work. The General Medical Council (GMC) which regulates all doctors in the UK states that:

> You must not use your professional position to pursue a sexual or improper emotional relationship with a patient or someone close to them. (GMC 2013: paragraph 53)

It is clear that any relationship with a patient, or with a patient's mother, would be a boundary violation (Galletly 2004), a breach of professional guidance and possibly subject to inquiry and sanction by the General Medical Council.

All of which makes it more curious that when Richard and Shula became romantically involved, no one thought about the seriousness of what had occurred. It is even more unlikely given that one of the people most devastated by the relationship between Richard and Shula was Usha Gupta who, as well as being the duped partner of Richard Locke, is also a solicitor and would, one might imagine, be well-versed in professional and regulatory standards. Indeed, the only person to mention the significant ethical breach by Dr Locke was the also-duped Alistair Lloyd who, on discovering the affair, accused Richard directly of using his professional position to take advantage of Shula when she was vulnerable during Daniel's illness. Dr Locke vehemently denied he had done any such thing.

Does it matter, though, what Dr Locke's intentions were or whether he perceived his behaviour to be unethical? The GMC, were it to have investigated Dr Locke's conduct and relationship with Shula, would be unlikely to be persuaded by his protestations. For a doctor who had cared for a bereaved woman at her most vulnerable and also been responsible for her child to have had a sexual relationship whilst both were registered as his patients is a serious breach of professional standards. Indeed, Dr Locke's objections and denial of the significance of his conduct may lead a hearing committee to conclude that he lacks insight and self-awareness, further exacerbating their concerns about his probity and professionalism.

There are other ways in which boundaries between professionals and patients can be blurred and challenged (Gabbard and Nadelson 1995). A useful distinction is between boundary crossings in which harm may not necessarily occur, and boundary violations in which harm does occur (Gutheil and Gabbard 1993). Self-disclosure, differential availability, attention or allocation of resource, mixing personal and professional contact, gifts, emotional involvement, financial transactions, time, 'rule-bending' and 'making exceptions' can all indicate that boundaries are becoming confused (Nadelson and Notman 2002). Most boundary violations do not occur suddenly, but are the culmination of progression in boundary pushing whereby a professional and his or her patient have become closer over a period of time; as was the case with Shula and Richard Locke. Boundary pushing, crossing and violating can come from any direction i.e. the patient may, consciously or otherwise, push the boundary with the clinician. However, the onus is on the healthcare professional to maintain boundaries. As such, it does not matter how much Shula may have flirted with, depended on, or encouraged Dr Locke; it was his responsibility to maintain the professional boundary.

As a rural doctor, Richard Locke does have particular challenges: he has dual relationships whereby he is both member of the community and doctor to those in that community. He is likely to encounter patients socially at village events and to be invited to parties and dinners with those whom he last saw in the surgery. The challenges and vulnerabilities of doctors who work in rural areas are well-documented (Graber 2011). As such, Dr Locke should, arguably, be even more aware of the need to negotiate boundaries carefully. Let's hope that at least some of his time in Manchester before he returned to Ambridge last year was spent on continuing professional development.

Carol's Confession

One of the more trying aspects of Carol Tregorran's return to Ambridge were the hints of a latent 'dark side' or, at least, a tendency to dabble in the magical. With her mysterious herbal teas, tendency to sense disquiet in others and oblique references to her recently deceased husband, it wasn't long before Jennifer Aldridge was pursuing her suspicions about the cause of John's death. The storyline culminated in an exchange between Carol and Jennifer in which they discussed the impact of John's illness and his suffering at the end of his life. The conversation was shrouded, one assumes deliberately, in ambiguity and suffused with euphemistic references. Nonetheless, there seemed to be at least the possibility that Carol had, in some way, assisted in John's death.

The question of assisted dying is one of the most vexed and recurring moral problems in medical ethics. At present, in the United Kingdom, it is illegal for anyone, whether professional or otherwise, to assist in, or cause, another person's death (Bowman 2011). There have been several attempts to change the law to permit assisted dying in prescribed circumstances, most recently in the form of Lord Falconer's Bill, but those efforts have failed (Dyer 2015). Alongside, the parliamentary attempts to change statute law, a number of high profile common law decisions about assisted dying have taken place in the courts including those in respect of Debbie Purdy, Tony Nicklinson and Paul Lamb (Mulloch 2015). Those cases have raised awareness of the moral arguments relating to assisted dying. However, the law has remained unchanged, although Debbie Purdy's case led to clarification regarding prosecution guidelines (Starmer 2014) in respect of those who help others to travel to, or make arrangements with, an overseas clinic in a jurisdiction where assisted dying is lawful, such as Dignitas in Switzerland.

The extent of Carol's involvement, if any, in John's death remains unclear. However, there were interesting shifts in Jennifer's response after she and Carol finally spoke about John's final moments. No longer was Jennifer on a crusade to obtain 'the truth'. Rather, she was in contemplative mode, recognizing perhaps that whatever 'the truth' might be, the complexities of claiming moral certainty over another's decision in the face of suffering were greater than she had previously considered.

There was, perhaps not unexpectedly, not much discussion of the moral concepts that generally inform debates about assisted dying such as the distinction between acts and omissions and the relevance of intention and foresight. Instead, a subsequent exchange with that great moral philosopher Lilian debated the contrasting ethical considerations in respect of what Carol may, or may not, have done. And, on that occasion, perhaps the drama was all the better for its deftness in respect of medical ethics.

Conclusion

Medical ethics is inherently concerned with disagreement. Its focus is the consideration of contested questions. As such, it is a rich source of drama. It is therefore surprising that it has not featured more in *The Archers* particularly given the prevalence of medical storylines. In the case of Dr Locke, the omission of ethics is an oversight that resulted in a cautionary tale for anyone learning about professional boundaries. In the case of Carol, its absence spared the listeners yet more of Jennifer's moralizing and conspiracy theories. For reasons of space, only two examples are discussed here, yet there have been, and will continue to be, many opportunities for the everyday story of ethics amongst country folk.

References

Bolton, J. (2000). 'How About Earning Points for Continuing Medical Entertainment?', *BMJ* 320: 1408.
Bowman, D. (2011). 'Death, Distress and Decisions: End of Life' in *The Worried Student's Guide to Medical Ethics and Law*. London: BPP Learning Media.
Brown, J. (2016). 'Domestic Abuse in The Archers: Putting the Storyline into Context', *British Politics and Policy at LSE* <http://blogs.lse.ac.uk/politicsandpolicy/> accessed 1 June 2016.

Dillon, R. (2013). *The Archers: An Unofficial Companion*. Chichester: Summersdale Publishers.

Dover, S. (1989). 'Doctor to the Archers', *BMJ* 299: 1623–5.

Dyer, C. (2015) 'Assisted Dying Bill is Defeated in the House of Commons by 330 to 118 Votes', *BMJ* 351: h4917.

Gabbard, G. O., and C. Nadelson (1995). 'Professional Boundaries in the Physician–Patient Relationship', *JAMA* 273.18: 1445–9.

Galletly, C. A. (2004). 'Crossing Professional Boundaries in Medicine: The Slippery Slope to Patient Sexual Exploitation', *MJA* 181.7: 380–3.

General Medical Council (2013). *Good Medical Practice*. London: GMC.

Graber, M. A. (2011). 'The Overlapping Roles of the Rural Doctor', *Virtual Mentor* 13.5: 273–7.

Gutheil, T. G., and G. O. Gabbard (1993). 'The Concept of Boundaries in Clinical Practice: Theoretical and Risk Management Dimensions', *The American Journal of Psychiatry* 150.2: 188–96.

Miller, B. (2015). *For the Love of The Archers*. Chichester: Summersdale Publishers.

Mulloch, A. (2015). 'The Assisted Dying Bill and the Role of the Physician', *Journal of Medical Ethics* 41: 621–4.

Nadelson, C., and M. T. Notman (2002). 'Boundaries in the Doctor–Patient Relationship', *Theoretical Bioethics* 23.3: 191–201.

Pywell, A. (2011). 'The Ways in which Dramas Affect Public Perceptions of Ageing', *Nursing Older People* 23.3: 26–8.

Starmer, K. (2014). 'Assisted Suicide Guidelines: Three Years On', *Medico-Legal Journal* 82.2: 48–56.

Stepney, R. (2011). 'A Series of Unfortunate Events? Morbidity and Mortality in a Borsetshire Village', *BMJ* 343: d7518.

Toye, J. (2009). *The Archers Miscellany*. London: BBC Books.

Review by Dr Richard Locke, Keeper's Cottage, Ambridge

Look, I don't mean to be rude, but I'm not sure what you're implying. I think I'm ethical and I'm taken aback you'd suggest otherwise. It's not easy, you know, being a doctor in a village like Ambridge. Of course I try to fit in and be sociable. It'd be odd if I didn't make the effort to be part of village life. A drink in The Bull or a game of cricket are all part and parcel of being a member of the community. Well yes, I do know that Shula was technically a patient. Dan, too. But you have to understand that no one in Ambridge is just a patient: they're also my neighbours and yes, often, my friends too. I'm always having to negotiate what I know about people when I see them socially, like Rob Titchener ... Anyway, never mind. It's not as if we planned it. God knows, if we could have avoided hurting people, we would have done. It is easy for others to gossip and to judge, but we genuinely cared about each other. Still do. To be frank, I resent the suggestion that it was somehow exploitative or 'inappropriate'. Anyway, a lot of water has passed under the bridge since then. I'm just grateful that Shula and I can be friends. And to see what a terrific young man Dan's become ... well, it's brilliant. I'm enjoying working in a group practice now too. It's good to have partners and other doctors around. I wonder where Lizzie is registered ...

SAMANTHA WALTON

Cider with Grundy: On the Community Orchard in Ambridge

This chapter explores the cultural and literary landscape of Ambridge through attention to the orchard. The practices of cider-pressing, wassailing, and drinking cider are all fundamental to village life. However, these traditions cannot be seen as uninterrupted, continuous, or unthreatened within the long history of Borsetshire. Since 1960, Britain has lost around two thirds of its orchards due to economic pressures, the rise of imported fruit, and changes in land use. In 1988, the environmental activist group Common Ground started the 'Save Our Orchards' campaign (Clifford and King n.d.), in which they attempted to spark interest in threatened orchards and urge communities to establish new ones. This hope was made a possibility with the new Community Right to Bid in 2011 (DCLG). Uncannily, within a month of the change in the law, Ambridge established its own community orchard, used for cider-pressing and rites and activities including wassailing and the Apple Day. This last festival was wholly invented by Common Ground as part of the Save Our Orchards campaign, and its purpose was to kindle communal and personal expressions about the meaning of nature-culture connections. Through attention to these contexts, I will read The Archers as a literature of place, reflective of histories of ecological and economic change in rural England, and of those cultural actions that sought to celebrate local distinctiveness and revive the notion of the orchard as a community asset and site of shared local knowledge and meaning.

Cider with Grundy

According to Ambridge lore, there's always been an orchard on Grange Farm land. It may have been established during the hey-day of cider making from late seventeenth to mid-eighteenth century (Clifford and King 2006: 92). After they lost the farm, Oliver Sterling let the Grundys continue collecting apples for cider-pressing. Aside from the yearly harvest, the orchard fell into neglect. Ed Grundy used it for grazing cattle, but the trees were uncared for, meaning non-cider varieties and perry-pears went to waste.

The idea of establishing a community orchard was hatched by Professor Jim Lloyd in late September 2011. On a 'golden afternoon', Jim volunteered to help Joe with the cider apple. To the background sound of bird song, Jim quoted the opening lines of John Keats's 1819 ode 'To Autumn':

Seasons of mist and mellow fruitfulness
Close bosom-friend of the maturing sun
Conspiring with him how to load and bless
With fruit the vines that round the thatch-eaves run.

'I think Keats must have imagined a scene just like this one when he wrote those lines', Jim mused. In answer, Joe suggested that Keats should have turned his talents to celebrating the local apple variety: 'I tell you what; he should have written a poem to the Borsetshire Beauty ... Makes the best cider of the lot of them'. This may risk reducing Keats to a mere forerunner of Ambridge Poet Laureate Bert Fry. However, the comparison between folk and urbane literatures gives us a clue as to how the community orchard will be poised from its beginning between distinct literary genres which reflect on human-nature relations. Romantic, pastoral, and georgic tropes are all discernible, while the activities of environmental arts charity Common Ground also contributed directly to *The Archers*' community orchard plot. Understood culturally and historically, *The Archers* can be seen as an environmental literature which has the potential to profoundly influence its listeners' attitudes human-nature relations and ecological interdependence. An examination of the different literatures that influenced representations of the community orchard will give a sense of how the scriptwriters are playing with different literary traditions in order to contribute to public debates about rural culture and the current environmental crisis.

Romanticism

Romanticism has become a byword for simplified, idealized depictions of the countryside. Listeners to *The Archers* are sometimes accused of having 'romanticized' attitudes to rural life, while snippets of Romantic verse are often quoted in rather superficial ways (sorry, Jim) to celebrate the beauty and balance of the natural world. In literary scholarship, the Romantic construction of 'Nature' as a sympathetic and beneficent deity has been criticized as a fantasy of bourgeois writers whose poetry obscured the exploitative economic relations and social destructiveness of the Agricultural and Industrial Revolutions (McGann 1983). However, from the 1990s onwards, environmental critics – *ecocritics* – rehabilitated the Romantics, arguing that their vision of 'Nature' was more complex, and might form the basis of more ethical and ecologically conscious relationships between humans and nature. For example, Keats wrote his ode 'To Autumn' during an exceptionally warm September, following three years of atrocious weather caused by the eruption of a volcano in Indonesia. To Jonathan Bate, '"To Autumn" is not an escapist fantasy [...] it is a meditation on how human culture can only function through links and reciprocal relations with nature. [...] [T]here is a direct correlation between the self's bond with its environment and the bonds between people that make up society' (2000: 257).

In the collaborative enterprise between Jim and the Grundys, local knowledge and affective ties combine with Jim's Romantic understanding of nature to develop the orchard as a site to build and strengthen bonds between nature, individuals, and the wider community. In the present context of environmental crisis, building such reciprocal links at the local level is essential, but must take place in the context of wider awareness of how one place inevitably connects to and affects other places. For Keats, an Indonesian volcano made links between human and natural flourishing apparent. For Ambridge residents, the impact of global ecological interconnectedness is felt in a variety of ways: Adam's innovations at Home Farm have forced some serious thinking about industrial agriculture and loss of soil fertility, while the flood sparked concern about river management, land development, and climate change. Romanticism, viewed as an ecological literature concerned with revealing the interdependence of culture and nature, is a more positive model for *The Archers* than the chocolate-box, sentimentalized genre of writing it is often mischaracterized as.

Georgic

As a classicist, we can assume that Jim's attitude to the countryside has been shaped by his knowledge of Virgil's *Georgics*. The *Georgics* is a long poem comprised of four cycles, written by the Roman poet in 29 BC. It meditates on the changing agricultural seasons, providing practical information about all aspects of rural life, from bee-keeping to fencing cornfields, grafting fruit trees to enriching soil. It doesn't idealize rural work or look at the lives of labourers through rose-tinted spectacles: it is upfront about the conflicts and challenges of rural life, ultimately emphasizing 'the importance of paying close attention to the natural world, of living harmoniously with animals and plants by practicing good stewardship' (Becker 2006: 43). The spirit of Virgil's *Georgics* can be felt in Jim's regret that the apples are going to waste, while a great deal of Classical virtue underpins his belief in responsible cultivation and productive husbandry. Luckily for the enterprise as a whole, Jim also put his classical training to good use when he diffused the first conflict encountered by the new Cider Club: how to divide the cider yield up, and whether the Grundys – as owners of the cider press – get extra. Jim's diplomatic solution might have been taken straight from the *Georgics*:

> Come then, and learn what tilth to each belongs
> According to their kinds, ye husbandmen,
> And tame with culture the wild fruits, lest earth
> Lie idle. (Virgil 1881: 35)

Save Our Orchards!

The orchard revival can also be seen as part of a wider response to environmental crisis and communal fragmentation in the context of rural modernity. Since 1960, Britain has lost around two-thirds of its orchards due to economic pressures, the rise of imported fruit, and changes in land use, particularly house and road development. Loss of orchards has meant a loss of habitats for wildlife and copious varieties of apples: 'Of the 2,000 culinary and dessert apples, and hundreds more cider varieties, which have been grown in this country, only a few handfuls are widely known and used today' (Clifford and King n.d.). The loss of orchards and apple varieties is threatening to biodiversity and crop resilience, and also to community identity through the loss of somewhere to work, socialize, collect produce and enact rites and rituals which connect people to places and environments. With the loss of orchards comes the loss of a cultural landscape and a lived 'taskscape': 'where the habitual practices of humans form familiar practices which can become landscapes or places' (Cloke and Jones 2000: 652).

Reviving the decaying Ambridge orchard took place in the context of environmental activism focused on the orchard and spearheaded by the environmental arts and activism group Common Ground, run by Sue Clifford and Angela King. After they had campaigned for orchards for twenty years, in August 2011 the government released a how-to guide on community orchards, which advised groups on how to negotiate new laws such as Community Right to Reclaim Derelict Land and Right to Bid (DCLG). The Guide quite rightly cites Common Ground as the instigators of the movement. Common Ground's *Save Our Orchards* campaign began in 1988, when they commissioned the photographer James Ravilious to produce a book and a touring exhibition titled *Orchards: Photographs of the West Country* (Ravilious 1989) These black-and-white images depict the charms of rural England; in one image – which could come straight out of the Fairbrothers' marketing material for Upper Class Eggs – sunlight streams through apple trees and falls on a brood of hens pecking in the grass, while in another, a May Queen sits amongst blossomed boughs in a scene recalling Lynda's Spring Pageant (or should that be *The Wicker Man*?). However, the images are also riven with conflict. Some depict trees being felled and burnt, while the 'Save Our Orchard!' posters displayed by campaigners suggests that these serene places and lively social spaces are under imminent threat.

Pastoral

It is the willingness of Ravilious to show the charms and challenges of orchards that mark his series as a complex, even georgic reflection on the real labour of orchard management. In contrast, we can look to an *Archers* plotline interwoven with the community orchard revival. In late summer 2011, Leonie Snell and James Bellamy headed to Borsetshire to write a book that captured everything 'villagey and quaint' about Ambridge, *A Little Bit of Heaven: A Year in the Life of a Country Village.* Their perspective on the rural is in keeping with another long – indeed, ancient – tradition of reflecting on the countryside: the pastoral. The pastoral genre was inaugurated in the Greek and Roman period and derived from the *Idylls* of Theocritus and *Eclogues* of Virgil. Although the Classical authors' works are not so simplistic as to fancifully idealize the rural, the 'pastoral ethic' they inaugurated finds expression in countless representations of bucolic, harmonious country life. The pastoral, in overview, represents a Golden Age of retreat from the troubles of city affairs: shepherds are warm and safe in their huts, the culverts aren't blocked and the pigs never escape. Like the Arcadia region in Greece which many pastorals reflect, Ambridge is 'the perfect location for a poetic paradise, a literary construct of a past Golden Age in which to retreat by linguistic idealization' (Gifford 2001: 20). This is exactly the kind of idyll that James and Leonie wanted to capture.

However, it is a project that has sensible Ambridge residents running for cover, because the village that James and Leonie imagine doesn't exist, and probably never did. The pastoral is thick with the aura of nostalgia and loss, and to capture Ambridge as they want to, James and Leonie have to edit out all those aspects that make it real, lived-in and modern. They want a picture of Ambridge frozen in time, a pastoral literature to sell as an imaginative 'retreat' for London readers. It was a clever plotline, a 'play within a play', in which the scriptwriters reminded listeners that *The Archers* invites complexity and conflict, and (although rural listeners may disagree on this) offers a more realistic representation of country life.

As the community orchard was established at the same time as James and Leonie were scoping out the village for shots, the newly established Cider Club had to be discreet, or risk being transformed into bucolic peasantry under the couple's lens. As Jim warned: 'We'll have to swear everyone to secrecy over the cider making otherwise they'll be down on us like bats out of hell'. By distancing the orchard from the pastoral, the script-writers aligned it with more complex literary traditions and the Common Ground campaigns that inspired it. This was achieved openly – for example, by scriptwriter Keri Davies inviting Sue Clifford to discuss tree-dressing on the *Archers* blog (2012) – and more subtly, through embedding the orchard in the Ambridge cultural landscape.

New Traditions

Since the community orchard was established, it's been used for tree dressing rituals, Apple Days and, in January 2016, a wassailing ceremony featuring Joe Grundy and Phoebe Tucker as wassail king and queen. During the wassail, local amateur historian Jennifer Aldridge discussed the pagan origins of the ritual, while Kirsty Miller, the incomer in this scenario, and Roy Tucker, correspondingly the local, tried to work out what on earth was going on as Phoebe was lifted into a tree with a slice of toast held to the chorus of the Borsetshire wassail. Whatever it is, Roy exclaimed, 'it's been going on for hundreds of years'.

Wassails are indeed medieval in origin, and have a root in both courtly and country traditions. However, although these practices are presented as fundamental to village life, the recent community orchard revival shows that these traditions cannot be seen as uninterrupted or continuous within the long history of Borsetshire. While wassailing apple trees in winter did continue for centuries in a few villages, the reason for Roy's sketchy knowledge of the ritual is that for Ambridge, wassailing is a 'new tradition'. Unsurprisingly, Common Ground popularized the revived ritual, which was nearly forgotten in much of the countryside. Like their hybrid, mul-ticultural tree dressing rituals (inspired by the Indian Chipko Movement) and the wholly invented Apple Day (now a popular UK-wide autumn festival), wassailing was seen by Common Ground as an event through which cultures and communities – in all their intricacy and variety – can be performed, explored, and strengthened, and in which human-nature interdependence could be acknowledged and celebrated.

The revival of wassailing says as much – perhaps more – about the future of human-nature relations than their history. Seen as a 'new' tradition', not a heritage piece, wassailing can attest to the complex, conflicted and far from idyllic history of British orchards. Wassailing's revival demonstrates how environments can be consciously changed through processes of reinterpretation and community co-production. Places should not remain static or be preserved in aspic; revived and newly invented rites can stimulate collective and individual expressions about the history and future of human–nature relationships, threats to environments and biodiversity loss, and the meaning and value of places in the present moment to the lives that depend on them.

References

Bate, J. (1995). 'The "Ode to Autumn"' as Ecosystem'. In L. Coupe (ed.), *The Green Studies Reader*. London: Routledge.

Becker, R. (2006). 'Timely Engagements: Summer and Sustainability in "The Georgics of Virgil"', *American Poetry Review* 35.6: 43–4.

Clare, John (2014 [1827]). 'February'. In E. Robinson, G. Summerfield and D. Powell (eds), *The Shepherd's Calendar*. Oxford. Oxford University Press.

Clifford, S., and A. King (2006). *Cider and Cider-Orchards: In England in Particular*. London: Hodder and Stoughton.

Clifford, S., and A. King (n.d.). *Save Our Orchards: Common Ground* <https://www.commonground.org.uk/save-our-orchards/> accessed 6 June 2016.

Cloke, P., and O. Jones (2000). 'Dwelling, Place, and Landscape: An Orchard in Somerset', *Environment and Planning A* 33.4: 649–66.

DCLG (2011). *Community Orchards: How To Guide* <https://www.gov.uk/government/uploads/system/uploads/attachment_data/file/11466/1973262.pdf> accessed 6 June 2016.

Davies, K. (2012). 'Tree-Dressing Day', *Archers Blog* <http://www.bbc.co.uk/blogs/thearchers/entries/45cf70a5-a35b-3852-a863-b2ba655884b5> accessed 6 June 2016.

Gifford, T. (2001). *Pastoral*. London and New York: Routledge.

Keats, John (1988 [1819]). 'To Autumn', in *The Complete Poems*, ed. J. Barnard. London: Penguin.

McGann, Jerome (1983). *The Romantic Ideology: A Critical Investigation*. Chicago: University of Chicago Press.

Philips, John (1708). *Cyder: A Poem in Two Books.* London: Jacob Tonson.

Ravilious, J. (1989). *The Orchard Archive: Common Ground* <https://www.common-ground.org.uk/james-ravilious/> accessed 6 June 2016.

Virgil (1881 [c. 29 BC]). *The Georgics of Virgil*, trans. J. Rhoades. London: Kegan Paul.

Review by Professor Jim Lloyd (University of Stirling, retired), Greenacres, Ambridge, Borsetshire

'Undique totis/usque adeo turbatur agris', so Virgil tells us in the *Eclogues*, and indeed, 'everywhere the whole land/Is in such turmoil', threatened by irrational building schemes and the scheming of predatory developers. Virgil's so-termed pastoral 'idyll' was also under threat of the machinations of Rome; just another element of his masterpiece that has been woefully misunderstood (although I do credit Dr Walton for acknowledging this distortion, and would ask that she add that the damage was done by sentimentalizing Victorians). As Saunders contends, the *Eclogues* are deeply concerned with 'absence, melancholy and loss' (2008: 3), which is exactly what I experienced seeing the apples wasted and the orchard lie idle. While Keats was indeed on my mind that day, perhaps Dr Walton should turn her attentions to more local poetic traditions. As I went on to explain to Joe, Bert Fry has a worthy ancestor in the peasant-poet John Clare: 'The mavis thrush with wild delight,/Upon the orchard's dripping tree,/Mutters, to see the day so bright,/Fragments of young Hope's poesy' (2014: 23); while in John Philips's 1708 poem 'Cyder', we find a far more detailed almanac of orchard management than Virgil was able to provide. Philips cautions against the damage caused by snakes, 'House-bearing Snails' and 'filthy Swine' that invade unguarded orchards (24–6). Indeed, on that note, the further we can keep James and Leonie and their saccharine fantasies away from the Cider Club, the better.

KATHERINE RUNSWICK-COLE

The Dis/appearance of Disability in *The Archers* ... or Why Bethany had to go to Birmingham

In this chapter, I will do four things. First, I will briefly introduce the reader to the context of my academic area of study: Critical Disability Studies. Second, I will consider the role of disability within cultural texts (books, films, television programmes and, indeed, radio drama) by drawing from the work of Mitchell and Synder (2000) and their idea of 'narrative prosthesis'. Third, I will examine the dis/appearance of disability in The Archers *with reference to the lives of three characters who have been identified as disabled people: Darrell Makepeace, Daniel Hebden Lloyd and Bethany Tucker. Finally, I will argue that the use of disability as narrative prosthesis, or device for developing the plot or characterisation of non-disabled characters, has obscured possibilities for engagement with the social, political and economic dimensions of disability.*

An Introduction to (Critical) Disability Studies

I locate my work in the field of critical disability studies. Disability studies are a relatively new academic discipline that began to emerge as a distinct area of academic inquiry in the 1990s (Mallett and Runswick-Cole 2014). Before the 1990s, in academia, disability was usually discussed in the contexts of medicine and psychology (Barnes 2008). Since then disability studies have emerged as an inter-disciplinary area of study, cutting across traditional divides with contributions to the field coming from psychology (Finkelstein 1980; Goodley 2011) sociology (Oliver 1990); education (Barton 1997; Slee 1997) feminist theory (Morris 1993) as well as literary theory and cultural studies (Mitchell and Snyder 2000).

These diverse contributions to the study of disability are united by their rejection of any understanding of disability that locates (the *problem* of) disability solely *within the person* (Albrecht et al. 2001). In contrast, (the *problem* of) disability is firmly understood as a *sociological* concept, located in the social world, rather than as an individual, biological deficit (Mallett and Runswick-Cole 2014).

In British disability studies, this focus on the sociological, rather than the biological nature of disability, is often underpinned by appeals to the social model of disability (Oliver 1990). A central claim of the social model of disability is that there is a distinction between impairment and disability: impairment: is the functional limitation within the individual caused by physical, mental or sensory impairment; disability: is the loss or limitation of opportunities to take part in the normal life of the community on an equal level with others due to physical and social barriers (Disabled People International 1982, as cited in Goodley 2011: 6). In this view, disability is a form of social oppression imposed on people with impairments in a disabling world, rather than a necessary result of the presence of impairment, per se.

Enter Critical Disability Studies

As a new area of academic inquiry, disability studies are constantly changing and developing. Recent change has included the emergence of Critical Disability Studies (Goodley 2011; Meekosha and Shuttleworth 2009). Critical disability studies aim to understand and to challenge exclusionary and oppressive practices associated with disablism and to consider the ways these intersect with other forms of marginalisation including hetero/sexism, racism, poverty and imperialism. Critical Disability Studies also seek to develop the study of disability in a number of ways: to challenge the dominance global North analyses within disability studies scholarship; to see the social model of disability as but one in a number of analytical tools; to welcome ideas from cultural studies and humanities (Goodley 2013, adapted from Mallett and Runswick-Cole 2014).

Cultural Studies and Narrative Prosthesis

It is Critical Disability Studies' engagement with cultural studies that is the focus here, specifically Mitchell and Schneider's (2001) concept of 'narrative prosthesis'. In their book *Narrative Prosthesis: Disability & the Dependencies of Discourse*, Mitchell and Snyder explore the pervasive use of disability in European and North American literature. They argue that, in cultural texts, disability serves as 'narrative prosthesis': a disabled character appears as a crutch to shore up the 'norm' somewhere else in the text. Take, for example, Berubé's (2005) discussion of Dickens's *A Christmas Carol*. In *A Christmas Carol*, the young 'crippled' boy, Tiny Tim, serves as a literary device to develop another character; Tiny Tim enables the miserly Scrooge to re-discover the human kindness within him and to gain redemption at the end of the narrative. The social and political dimensions of disability are obscured as Tiny Tim's primary function is not to condemn the treatment of 'crippled' children in Victorian England, but rather to facilitate the reclamation of Scrooge's moral worth (Bérubé 2005).

Narrative Prosthesis and *The Archers*

So, informed by Mitchell and Snyder's work, I seek to examine the function of the dis/appearance of disability in *The Archers*. I've written elsewhere about how disability is made visible or invisible in order to support the narrative arc; in Channel 4's *Benefits Street* disability appears and disappears to support the 'benefit scrounger' storyline (Runswick-Cole and Goodley 2015). Here, I explore the dis/appearance of disability in *The Archers* as narrative prosthesis with particular reference to three characters' relationships with disability: Darrell Makepeace, Dan Hebden Lloyd and Bethany Tucker.

Darrell Makepeace

Interestingly, given Berubé's (ibid.) discussion of Tiny Tim, the decline of Darrell Makepeace has been described as containing all the elements of a classic Dickensian morality tale (Henderson 2013). Darrell made a series of 'bad choices' from being led astray by workmates into receiving stolen goods and being imprisoned. His marriage broke up and he became homeless. This combination of events led to him engaging, sporadically, with mental health services. It could be argued that Darrell's storyline offers a timely social commentary on welfare cuts, mental health and community inclusion (Goodley and Runswick-Cole 2014; Henderson 2013).

Darrell was a newcomer to the village and his time in Ambridge was relatively short lived. Nonetheless, his temporary presence served an important role as narrative prosthesis; when homeless Darrell was offered a bed at The Stables, the home of Shula Hebden Lloyd, Darrell's troublesome presence as a houseguest allowed the erstwhile 'St Shula of Ambridge' to assert her saintly credentials. While Darrell exasperated Shula, his presence allowed her, yet again, to demonstrate her compassion and moral worth. Disability appeared and then disappeared to shore up Shula's claim for beatification, while an opportunity for an engagement with the socio-political aspects of disability, through sustained engagement with the issues faced by mental health service users in a time of austerity, was lost.

Dan Hebden Lloyd

In contrast to the temporary residence of Darrell in Ambridge, Daniel Hebden Lloyd (or Dan, as we must now respectfully call him) has been a core member of the extended Archer family for the last twenty-one years. However, while Dan's character is a fixed presence in rural Ambridge, disability was a temporary presence in his life; it appeared and then disappeared. As a child, Dan lived with juvenile arthritis. Dan's impairment played a crucial role in plot development; it facilitated a (not so saintly) liaison between Shula, Dan's mother, and Richard Locke, their GP. Disability was made present in the storyline only so long as was necessary to bring Shula and Richard together, and to create the chaos that ensued with their partners, Alistair and Usha respectively. Yet again, an opportunity to move beyond a brief awareness raising campaign about the medical nature of childhood arthritis, and to engage in a sustained way with the political and cultural contexts of childhood disability, was lost.

And so Bethany had to go to Birmingham ...

And so when Bethany Tucker was born on 16 January 2013, given the permanent nature of her impairment, Down Syndrome, with the benefit of the present analysis, it seemed inevitable that her residence in Ambridge would be only temporary. When Bethany was born, the storyline offered a sensitive portrayal of the issues facing new parents of disabled children. Information about sources of support was posted on the *Archers* blog. The scriptwriters didn't pull their punches in their portrayal of Peggy's discriminatory attitudes – the every-day disablism she exhibited outside the community shop was horribly familiar to many parents of disabled children, like me. As Bethany's parents, Mike and Vicky, were well-established characters, it seemed that Bethany would grow up in Ambridge alongside her peers. However, by the time Bethany was ready to start pre-school, it was clear that this was not to be the case. Instead, yet again, the presence of disability served as a prosthetic device, this time in order to explain the inexplicable: why Mike, who loved Ambridge, had lived in the village for years with family and friends around him, would leave and go to Birmingham.

Loxley Barratt Primary School 'could not cope with a child like Bethany', Vicky, her mother, told us; disability meant that *they had to go to Birmingham*, to get the 'specialist' help Bethany needed. There was no opportunity to discuss the possibility of inclusive education in rural Borsetshire – Bethany simply had to go to Birmingham.

Conclusion

Darrell, Dan and Bethany are not the only disabled characters to have made a temporary appearance in Ambridge. Brian Aldridge lives with epilepsy although it is rarely never mentioned; Jack Woolley's dementia, for the most part, disappeared into The Laurels nursing home with him, although Peggy, his wife, remained to give a carer's account; Christopher Carter made a miraculous recovery from a devastating injury that allowed Alice, his wife, to re-commit to her marriage and to living in Ambridge; Elizabeth Archer's heart condition is referenced only sporadically.

Amazingly, among the established families in Ambridge (the Archers, the Aldridges, the Grundys and the Carters), there is no one who identifies as a disabled person. In Ambridge, disability always and only emerges as a temporary phenomenon, smoothing the plot development or nurturing characterization. So far, any opportunity that has appeared for a sustained, everyday engagement with the ordinary day-to-day lives of disabled people has been lost.

So does the dis/appearance of disability in *The Archers* matter? It does. There is ever-increasing evidence that shows that cultural representations of disability have very 'real' impacts on the lives of disabled people (Inclusion London 2011). In the context of austerity and cuts to public services and welfare benefits, the rise of the 'scrounger' discourse, which positions disabled benefits claimants as a drain on the system, has coincided with a rise in reported hate crime on grounds of disability (Inclusion London 2011). Disabled people appear in the media as victims of crime and of horrific abuse and neglect, often at the hands of those meant to care for them. See, for example, the BBC's *Panorama* programme on Winterbourne View (BBC 2011; Green et al. 2015). While it is clearly important to document and to challenge the abuse of disabled people, if these are the only images we see of disabled people, this only serves to reinforce negative images of vulnerability that ultimately de-humanize disabled people.

And so it seems that it is high time for Bethany to return to Ambridge and to live a long and happy life in the bosom of her extended family, experiencing the ups and downs of life in an everyday story of country folk.

Acknowledgements

I would like to thank Rebecca Mallett, Jenny Morris and Lucy Rutherford for their helpful comments on this chapter.

References

Albrecht, G., K. D. Seelman and M. Bury (2001). 'Introduction: The Formation of Disability Studies'. In G. Albrecht, K. D. Seelman and M. Bury (eds), *Handbook of Disability Studies*. London: Sage: 1–10.

Barnes, C. (2008). *Disability and the Academy: A British Perspective* <http://disability-studies.leeds.ac.uk/files/library/Barnes-paris-presentation.pdf> accessed 1 December 2011.

Barton, L. (1997). 'Inclusive Education: Romantic, Subversive or Realistic?', *International Journal of Inclusive Education* 1.3: 231–42.

BBC (2011). Panorama: Under Cover Care, Abuse Exposed. BBC 1, reporter: Paul Kenyon.

Bérubé, M. (2005). 'Disability and Narrative', *PMLA* 120.2: 568–76.

Bury, M. (1997). *Health and Illness in a Changing Society*. London: Routledge.

Channel 4 (2014). *Benefits Street*, dir. Richard McKerrow. Love Productions.

Finkelstein, V. (1980). *Attitudes and Disabled People: Issues for Discussion*. New York: World Rehabilitation Fund.

Goodley, D. (2011). *Disability Studies: An Interdisciplinary Introduction*. London: Sage.

Goodley, D. (2013). 'Dis/entangling Critical Disability Studies', *Disability & Society* 28.5: 631–44.

Goodley, D., and K. Runswick-Cole (2014). 'Big Society? Disabled People with the Label of Learning Disabilities and the Queer(y)ing of Civil Society', *Scandinavian Journal of Disability Research*. DOI: 10.1080/15017419.2014.941924.

Green, B., A.-M. Bruce, P. Finn, A. Wright, D. Daniel, J. Povey and D. Repper (2015). *Independent Review of Deaths of People with a Learning Disability or Mental Health Problem in Contact with Southern Health NHS Foundation Trust April 2011 to March 2015* <https://www.england.nhs.uk/south/wp-content/uploads/sites/6/2015/12/mazars-rep.pdf> accessed 20 May 2016.

Henderson, L. (2013). 'Hard Times in *The Archers* at Christmas' <http://www.costofliving.net/hard-times-in-the-archers-at-christmas/>.

Inclusion London (2011). *Bad News for Disabled People: How Newspapers are Report-ing Disability* <http://www.inclusionlondon.co.uk>.

Mallett, R., and K. Runswick-Cole (2014). *Approaching Disability: Critical Issues and Perspectives*. Abingdon: Routledge.

Meekosha, H., and R. Shuttleworth (2009). 'What's so Critical about Critical Dis-ability Studies?', *Australian Journal of Human Rights* 15.1: 47–75.

Morris, J. (1993). 'Feminism and Disability'. *Feminist Review* 43: 57–70.

Mitchell, D., and S. Synder (2000). *Narrative Prosthesis: Disability and the Dependen-cies of Discourse (Corporealities: Discourses of Disability)*. Ann Arbor: University of Michigan Press.

Oliver, M. (1990). *The Politics of Disablement*. Basingstoke: Macmillan.

Runswick-Cole, K., and D. Goodley (2015). 'DisPovertyPorn: *Benefits Street* and the Dis/ability Paradox', *Disability & Society*, online early view <http://dx.doi.org /10.1080/09687599.2015.1008294>.

Slee, R. (1997) 'Imported or Important Theory? Sociological Interrogations of Disable-ment and Special Education', *British Journal of Sociology of Education* 18.3: 407–19.

Review by Vicky Tucker, Birmingham

Having Bethany has been such a surprise to us! She's full of sur-prises, our little Bethany, as I told Mike just the other day, when I caught her with her hand in the biscuit jar! I never thought we'd have a baby and if you'd told me that we'd have our Beth and leave Ambridge, I wouldn't have believed you. It's true, I loved Ambridge, had great friends there, especially lovely Lynda Snell, but after we had Beth, it didn't feel right any more. Peggy's com-ments outside the village shop didn't help. I don't think she knows much about a 'social model of disability'! I know all the family was in Ambridge but Roy (and Hayley) had their own lives, we couldn't ask them for help with Beth. Bethany would have been the first child with Down Syndrome to go to Loxley Barratt Primary School, and I didn't want that. I didn't want them learning how to do 'inclusive education' on our Beth, I wanted specialist help and Birmingham is the place for that. We live near the children's hospital now which was a godsend when Beth was in hospital with respiratory problems just recently. And if we'd stayed in Ambridge, as the only disabled person living there, who would she have had to look up to, to look at and say 'I could do that'? In Birmingham, I've got a support group for other parents of disabled children to help me. I'd never have had that in Ambridge. Perhaps if there had been other disabled people, other families with disabled children living there, I could have stayed but there weren't and there aren't, and Mike and I had to put our Bethany first and we did, and that's why we went to Birmingham.

NICOLA HEADLAM, WITH CARA COURAGE
AND PETER MATTHEWS

Conclusion: *Academic Archers* as a Fine-Detailed, Open, Cross-Disciplinary Space

> What is it that gets co-produced in nature and society? Are the most useful insights about co-production to be discovered at the level of science, power and culture writ large? Or is it more illuminating to trace in fine-detail how social worlds ... have gained stability and coherence, along with particular expressions of knowledge.
>
> — JASANOFF (2004: 5)

As discussed in the Introduction, *Academic Archers* was the first such event ever held. Standing in front of the assembled audience was a crystallizing and exposing experience. In this concluding chapter we argue that our instinctive approach to the co-production of the event, through the blending of speakers with formal credentials with an audience with infinite knowledge of life in Ambridge, led to a very fruitful space for dialogue. We suggest that the difference in tone and emphasis from normal academic shop-window-type conferences has implications that ought to resonate more widely.

As well as exploring the motivations of the organizers and participants we argue that a number of different things came together to raise *The Archers* into the public consciousness making the conference, and this book, particularly resonant in contemporary Britain. There has been a convergence of: first, social media engagement; second, desynchronized listening facilitated by podcasts and download; third, the stewardship of the controversial Sean O'Connor, which in turn led to the storyline of the abusive relationship between Rob and Helen Titchener (*née* Archer) that has both gripped and appalled the faithful and attracted new listeners. The storyline features heavily in the chapters in this volume.

As discussed in the Introduction to this collection, all three editors have a long-standing relationship with *The Archers*. However, it was largely a private and guilty pleasure. Nicola Headlam and Peter Matthews rarely discussed their daily dose with friends or colleagues, despite being as familiar with the intricate lineage of all the main clans – Archers, Aldridges, Grundys – as, well, family. (Cara Courage is an exception to this and would – and does – talk openly to everyone about *The Archers*, whether they are fans or not.) This life-long relationship is part of an inheritance, like support for a football team. This, we discovered, chatting to our authors and attendees on the day, was not unusual, with *The Archers* commonly being part of the intimate wallpaper of childhood.

As a result the contributors to this book have dealt with *The Archers* in different ways, as well as fusing the scholarly concerns of their own disciplines with storylines and themes. They are combined, however, in the best traditions of fandom research from cultural studies, where 'fandom research is best seen as an open-cross-disciplinary space for grappling with the highly various consequences of being a more than casual interpreter of a text' (Gray, Sandvoss and Lee Harrington 2007: 141).

Twitterati

As Lyn Thomas highlighted in her chapter, the fandom of *The Archers* is increasingly mobilized through social media, and the various Facebook groups and the *Omnibus* live tweetalong on a Sunday morning (#thearchers). As we discussed in the Introduction, as well as using Twitter for research purposes, the editors of this collection 'met' through contributing to the live tweetalong.

Behind such fandom lies a complex ecosystem of devotees with tribes as discrete as the village families themselves, using technology such as noticeboards, as well as more recent social media. These include: 'Mustardland' (established in 2005, a year after Facebook first launched on the campus of Harvard); *The Archers Anarchists* (who do not refer to SLs or SWs – storylines or scriptwriters – as they maintain that Ambridge is real); myriad

Facebook groups, such as *The Archers Addicts*, *Ambridge Addicts*, *Archers Anonymous* (and never the twain shall meet); fanchats on sites such as Mumsnet; and now *Academic Archers*.

A further feature has been the development of brilliant fan fiction, by the likes of the podcast *Dumteedum* and *The Ambridge Observer*. On Twitter we have Ambridge Synthetics (@ThePlarchers, *The Archers* in PlayMobile) and Alternative Archers (@AlternateArcher), the inner-monologue of characters delivered with unnerving accuracy in 140 characters. This also lends itself to a form of Twitter slash fiction, with most characters have one (if not more) Twitter accounts purporting to be them. In the wake of the Helen and Rob storyline a plethora of new accounts emerged, such as Peggy Woolley (@Peggy_Woolley), Baby Jack Archer (@TitchenerBaby) and Anna Tregorran (@annatregorran), which led to a quite bizarre blending of fact and fiction through the @BBCTheArchers handle and tweets from Keri Davies (@keridavies), a main scriptwriter. You will find a number of astute reviews of Grey Gables on TripAdvisor too. All of this activity points towards a highly creative and reflexive fandom, not only following conventional BBC Radio 4 demographics by being educated and affluent, but also being irreverent, imaginative and expert. As a result the BBC actively curate and mediate this space, encouraging listeners to share, chatting to them on Twitter and providing depth of content to embellish storylines, such as the Ambridge weather reports that appeared on the BBC website during the floods.

Podcasts

Much has been written on the cultural history of the radio itself, or, in even more retro mode, the wireless. As Thompson and Biddle (2013: 185) suggest:

> in this intimate relationship the radio is not only a facilitator of connections within imagined communities but is as an agent, a proxy for those communities, the radio itself is figured as 'company' as shorthand for its role as the tool. Solitary listening does not, then, imply solitude as such, as the notion of other listeners is [...] part of listening.

While some feared the internet would be the death knell for radio, it has found a resurgence through podcasts. Because of restrictions on music licensing these were often spoken-word, with *The Archers* and much of BBC Radio 4's output being some of the earliest podcasts the BBC produced. With investment in the iPlayer, this has changed who listens, and how and when they listen to *The Archers*. Fans from across the world can download the podcasts, and people in the UK can listen at any time after the first broadcast at 7.02pm. This offers opportunities for *The Archers* to play a more central role in people's lives. Nicola Headlam's earlier blasé take-it-or-leave it attitude to listening has been replaced by avid follow-up when work commitments take her away from the kitchen. For Peter Matthews this new way of listening has included downloading the *Omnibus* during a road-trip through the Canadian Rockies to catch-up on 'typhoid-Clarrie' and the E. coli breakout. It allowed Cara Courage to 'introduce' *The Archers* to her American housemates as an act of cultural understanding.

Editors and Scriptwriters

Sean O'Connor became editor of *The Archers* in 2013, taking over from Vanessa Whitburn, moving from the popular BBC television soap opera *EastEnders*. His storylines have caused controversy for being too sensationalist. Former UK Home Secretary David Blunkett told the *Radio Times* that '[u]nder new management – new editor, new writers – I fear that *The Archers* is on the verge of becoming the disappearing soap. *Coronation Street* and *EastEnders* must be rubbing their hands' (*The Radio Times* 2014).

However, O'Connor defended his decisions, explaining how *The Archers* is 'the only soap opera that is a multi-layered class structure. All the others feature different gradations of working class. And in the sense that the Shakespearian histories are about England, *The Archers* is about how we were, who we were, and who we could be. It's about the land and land is about our identity as British people' (*The Telegraph* 2014). However, in the storyline of Rob and Helen he held up a mirror to an uglier side of our society.

Helen and Rob

In the storyline of the abuse by Rob Titchener of his partner, and then wife, Helen, *The Archers* fandom had been treated to a more or less totally unprecedented storyline that has run over years, which had divided faithful escapist listeners as to its suitability and hooked in a new audience of those following the affair, courtship, marriage and capitulation of a once strong female character, resulting in an abusive and controlling relationship. The story has electrified listeners – revolting some – and was drip-fed in the most startling and intimate fashion.

It was in this context that the *Academic Archers* conference came about. The day itself became an exercise in co-produced research. The editors share research interests – largely in urban policy and practice – but also a healthy scepticism towards the idea that in our roles as experts we have any kind of monopoly of wisdom on the subjects in which we claim expertise. Co-production, whether in urban redevelopment and regeneration policy (Peter Matthews), art in the urban environment (Cara Courage), or the ways in which research may be mobilized to support policy processes (Nicola Headlam), serves to disturb some of the binaries and boundaries between the subject and object of knowledge, not to mention the privileging of certain forms of expertise.

As mentioned in our Introduction, it became apparent that *Archers* listeners are a certain type of lived expertise. While all presenters were used to presenting their research in teaching and academic environments (conferences, seminars etc.) and receiving questions on the intellectual content of their work, the expertise here was quite different. Questions referred to storylines from twenty or even thirty years ago, often before the presenters were even born, seeking academic clarification of inconsistencies. Many speakers were stumped by questions along the lines of 'What would [this character] think of this?' Fact and fiction blended to bizarre effect as questioners pointed out that it was not like that in their bit of the English countryside, so it could not be like that in Ambridge. And we all stopped at 2:03pm to listen to the broadcast on BBC Radio 4. What marked the day out for most of the academic speakers (except William Barras – he maintains socio-linguistics conferences are all like this; linguistics is where the party is at!) was that the day was spent laughing joyously and demonstrating our shared love for this programme. With the contemporary focus in universities in the UK on 'public engagement', 'outreach' and 'impact', the conference, and now this book, present a new way to engage the wider public in creating knowledge about contemporary society and the world. We therefore leave you with the comments of those who attended, attesting to this unique, co-produced, cross-disciplinary academic event:

> *I just wanted to say thank you for organizing yesterday – I had a lovely, lovely day, and you should all be proud of being responsible for such a successful event. It's no mean feat to keep an entire room engaged and interested through an entire day, including the afternoon slot! It was also great to have so many different disciplines represented. I really liked that variety, and again, it's a rare thing to have that spread of interests at a conference.*

> *I'd like to thank you and your colleagues for organizing such a tremendous event. It was thoroughly enjoyable, with an excellent programme, built towards appropriate climaxes at each break, and treated of some very profound themes. It was great to see the way the presenters took seriously the questions and processes without taking themselves – or The Archers – too seriously.*

> *Thank you everyone for such wonderful papers, and congratulations to the organizers for putting together such an engaging, hilarious and truly interdisciplinary day. I was really happy to be involved, and humbled by The Archers expertise in the room!*

> *A very unusual conference – the interdisciplinarity linked by a fictional text really worked. And the audience just loved it. Quite an achievement as Archers fans can be very critical!*

> *The energy and encounters coming out the day are what conferences should be about. A fun-filled, focused, interdisciplinary, critical celebration.*

> *The range of presentations and subject matter were outstanding and so humorous and some touched with sadness. There were many sobering issues dealt with in such an informative light way. Obviously using a soap as a medium to deliver education is clearly the way forward in education. I must remember this for my own undergrads and postgrads.*

> *It was great to take part in such a fascinating set of interdisciplinary discussions and to be able to talk to such an enthusiastic audience!*

> *I learned a lot and laughed a lot, which is a fantastic combination.*

Your conference showed academics have got a sense of humour and don't take themselves too seriously.

It was a fabulous day. I've been talking about it ever since!

The conference was just brilliant! A remarkable and memorable day!

A brilliant idea! I look forward to attending events in the future!

Thank you so much for making this happen.

Telling everyone I went to an Archers conference seems to be making me very popular, everyone wanting to know what it was like. I think, 25 years after we left school, it might be safe to be out to my school friends about it, now they've all become listeners too ...

References

Academic Archers <https://www.facebook.com/groups/AcademicArchers/> accessed 7 July 2016.

Alternative Archers (@AlternateArcher) <https://twitter.com/alternatearcher> accessed 7 July 2016.

Ambridge Addicts <https://www.facebook.com/groups/ambridgeaddicts/> accessed 7 July 2016.

Ambridge Synthetics (@ThePlarchers) <https://twitter.com/theplarchers> accessed 7 July 2016.

Archers Anarchists <http://www.archersanarchists.com> accessed 7 July 2016.

Anna Tregorran (@annatregorran) <https://twitter.com/annatregorran> accessed 7 July 2016.

Archers Anonymous <https://www.facebook.com/groups/690355214394535/> accessed 7 July 2016.

Baby Jack Archer (@TitchenerBaby) <https://twitter.com/titchenerbaby> accessed 7 July 2016.

BBC (n.d.). *Here's your Passport to Ambridge!* <http://www.bbc.co.uk/programmes/articles/1DrHJwj3ZolhjPzyMs7JQwz/heres-your-passport-to-ambridge> accessed: 29 June 2016.

Davies, K. (@keridavies) <https://twitter.com/keridavies> accessed 7 July 2016.

Dumteedum (podcast) <http://dumteedum.com> accessed 7 July 2016.

Gray, A., C. Sandvoss and C. Lee Harrington (2007). *Fandom: Identities and Communities in a Mediated World*. New York: New York University Press.

Grey Gables Hotel, Trip Advisor <https://www.tripadvisor.co.uk/Hotel_Review-g186402-d7295523-Reviews-Grey_Gables_Hotel-Birmingham_West_Midlands_England.html> accessed 7 July 2016.

Jasanoff, S. (2004). *States of Knowledge: The Co-Production of Science and the Social Order*. London: Routledge.

Radio Times (2014). 'Has the Archers Gone too Far?' (15–21 November).

The Ambridge Observer <http://ambridgeobserver.blogspot.co.uk> accessed 7 July 2016.

The Archers (@BBCthearchers) <https://twitter.com/BBCTheArchers> accessed 7 July 2016].

The Telegraph (2014). 'Sean O'Connor: The Man who "Sexed Up" *The Archers*' <http://www.telegraph.co.uk/culture/tvandradio/11172659/Sean-OConnor-The-man-who-sexed-up-the-Archers.html> accessed 29 June 2016.

Thompson, M., and I. Biddle (2013). *Sound, Music, Affect: Theorizing Sonic Experience*. London: Bloomsbury.

UK Weather Warning: Borsetshire, BBC website <http://www.bbc.co.uk/programmes/articles/4gnZoYZDdJW2NHHZ1vYzooy/uk-weather-warning-borsetshire> accessed 7 July 2016.

Woolley, P. (@Peggy_Woolley) <https://twitter.com/peggy_woolley> accessed 7 July 2016.

Review by Elizabeth Pargetter, Lower Loxley Hall, Am Vale, Borsetshire

Oh, things just haven't been the same since Roy left. I've been trying to keep on top of things, but it seems this just fell through. The ballroom was free on 17 February; I just checked the bookings. I must have missed the email from Dr Peter Matthews. It sounds like it was such an interesting day and *so* much fun. Living in the Am Vale, we do suffer from regular outages in the broadcasts of BBC Radio 4 between 2.03pm and 2.15pm and 7.03pm and 7.15pm Monday to Friday and every Sunday morning. It is very odd how regular it is. Therefore I don't really know what they're talking about when they mention 'The Archers'. Oh well, *Desert Island Discs* gave me some consolation after Nigel's death, so I understand what they mean about being a fan of Radio 4. Shuttling Lily and Freddie around Borsetshire, I often miss my favourite programmes on Radio 4, so it is very useful to be able to download them and catch-up. *The Food Programme* has been particularly useful when I consider how to develop the vineyard and the Orangery. However, I do find it very odd that so many people on Twitter send messages to @LizziePargetter and seem to know so much about my life. How did they find out about me and Roy in such detail? It must have been Susan Carter talking in the shop. Anyway, this has all reminded to update the booking system on the website. I must not miss opportunities to host academic events like this in future!

Notes on Contributors

WILLIAM BARRAS is Lecturer in Linguistics at the University of Aberdeen. He has research interests in dialectology, sociolinguistics and phonology. His PhD research investigated rhoticity and intrusive-r in East Lancashire. He also worked on the Fisherspeak project at the University of Aberdeen, documenting loss of vocabulary in the fishing dialects of the East Coast of Scotland. A formative *Archers* experience was sitting in the car at Rosemarkie beach, north of Inverness, listening to Tony Archer discovering John's tractor accident. Unfortunately BBC Radio 4 and BBC Radio Scotland used the same frequency, so this heart-breaking scene was underscored by Jimmy Shand's band playing in the background.

DEBORAH BOWMAN is Professor of Clinical and Mental Health Ethics at the Tavistock and Portman NHS Trust and Honorary Professor of Bioethics, Clinical Ethics and Medical Law at St George's, University of London. Her academic interests concern moral distress, therapeutic relationships and public involvement in ethical debate. She is an accredited mediator, specializing in healthcare conflict. The health humanities are a particular interest, especially theatre, and she is the editor of *Medical Humanities*. She is a regular commentator on a range of programmes, especially for BBC Radio 4. She has listened to *The Archers* since she was ten years old.

HELEN M. BURROWS is a Registered Social Worker and practice educator who is currently working as a Domestic Abuse Support Worker in Nottinghamshire. Until recently she was a lecturer in social work; she also researches the use of digital technology. Born the same year as Shula and Kenton, Helen grew up seeing Phil and Jill Archer as 'extra parents', and has followed her namesake's story with keen personal and professional interest. She is also a volunteer library assistant and is looking forward to lending out this book from her local Community Managed Library.

PHILIPPA BYRNE is a British Academy Postdoctoral Fellow at the University of Oxford, where she is also a tutor in medieval history at Somerville College. She received her DPhil from the University of Oxford in 2015 for a thesis on the duties of secular and ecclesiastical judges in medieval England. She has published on a number of aspects of medieval law and theology, in addition to writing about how medieval historians can engage with the public and bring the discipline to a wider audience. A trained lawyer, she currently works on concepts of government, community and justice across twelfth- and thirteenth-century Europe, and particularly in southern Italy and Sicily. She is a third-generation listener to *The Archers*, although she would like to stress that she has very little in common with her namesake, Pip Archer, and absolutely no interest in robotic milking. Having long searched for a way to combine her passion for the medieval world, BBC radio drama and the history of socialism, she is thrilled that the *Academic Archers* conference and this publication gave her the opportunity to do so.

CLEMENCY COOPER is Community Archaeology Manager for Oxford Archaeology, having previously worked for the British Museum and at the University of Cambridge as administrator for Carenza Lewis's unit from 2010 to 2014. Latterly brought up in Lincolnshire, she has listened to *The Archers* for as long as she can remember.

CARA COURAGE is an arts and placemaking researcher, practitioner, curator and writer. She has recently completed her PhD thesis, 'Making Places: Performative Arts Practices in the City', at the University of Brighton. Her research interests span the arts and the urban, in relation to co-production, arts practice and process, civic participation and social movements and the arts and city space and place. She is a member of the Placemaking Leadership Council, Fellow of the RSA and Academician of Academy of Urbanism and has founded a number of arts and architecture publications. She is a writer for both national and sector publications. Her relationship with *The Archers* is best summed up by the title of the talk she gives, 'My BDSM Relationship with *The Archers*', telling of both the pleasure and pain of being a devoted fan.

NICOLA HEADLAM is an adaptable and interdisciplinary urbanista whose work is on the governance, management and leadership of cities. Her research interest in the implementation of policy in the subnational UK began when she worked as a local government officer and led to a PhD at the Centre for Urban Policy Studies at the University of Manchester. Post-doctorally she was based at the Heseltine Institute for Public Policy and Practice at the University of Liverpool where her research took on a more futuristic hue with project work on cities and public policy through to the year 2065. Since 2015 she has been a Knowledge Exchange Fellow working within the Government Office for Science and the Urban Transformations portfolio at the University of Oxford. She visits Ambridge most days to escape all that.

CARENZA LEWIS is an archaeologist and Professor for the Public Understanding of Research at the University of Lincoln. Specializing for twenty-five years in medieval rural settlement studies, she has worked in government archaeology and as an academic at the University of Birmingham and the University of Cambridge. In 1994 she became one of the original presenters of Channel 4's *Time Team*, remaining with the series until 2004 when she set up a heritage outreach unit at the University of Cambridge, which she ran until moving to Lincoln in 2015. She was introduced to *The Archers* by a boyfriend while an undergraduate in the 1980s.

NEIL MANSFIELD is Professor of Design Engineering and Human Factors at Imperial College London. He is an expert in designing vehicles so that they are comfortable healthy environments and can get the best possible performance out of their users. Good design means that seats fit the drivers and that controls are easy and efficient to use, even if the task is very complex. He works with many sectors from planes, trains and automobiles, through to mining, military and agriculture. He has an experimental approach working with real users in the Human Performance and Experience laboratory, but, in common with many Ambridge characters, loves working in the field.

PETER MATTHEWS is Senior Lecturer in Social Policy at the University of Stirling. He has a research interest in urban inequalities and how policy can either exacerbate or tackle these. Recent research includes a review of the impact of middle-class activism, and the links between poverty and social networks. He is an editor of the journal *Local Government Studies* and leader of the Public Services and Governance research group. He started listening to *The Archers* about eight years ago when he found himself locked in his boyfriend's flat on a Sunday morning.

LAUREN MORGAN is a Human Factors Research Fellow and Lecturer at the University of Oxford. Her work is focused on ensuring the human is considered in all aspects of design, specifically when there are conflicts and pressures which is often the case in agriculture. She works across a variety of industries, and currently specializes in patient safety in health-care. She grew up on the family farm in mid-Wales, and so has experienced first-hand many of the issues and opportunities faced by modern farming today.

JO MORIARTY is a Senior Research Fellow at King's College London. She has a longstanding interest in support for older people and family carers and the relationship between paid and unpaid care. She has undertaken research into a wide range of topics, including ethnicity and ageing, social work education, and workforce recruitment and retention. She has also authored or co-authored a number of resources summarizing research findings for practitioners. She has edited the Innovative Practice section of the journal *Dementia* since it began publication in 2002. Growing up in a household where listening to *The Archers* was part of the daily routine, it has been a huge source of pride for her to be involved in this publication.

ABI PATTENDEN is an independent scholar. She completed her MA at the University of Exeter, following a BA in English and Drama. Her key areas of interest include representations of gender, and of friendship and romantic love, within Shakespearean comedy, structuralism, and conventions within Elizabethan and Jacobean theatre. She is on an extended break from academia and currently runs a successful business. She retains a keen interest in drama, and tweets and blogs about the connections she finds between Shakespeare and *The Archers* as @muchadoambridge. She is delighted to be involved in *Academic Archers*; it feels very appropriate, as she became a true addict whilst writing her MA thesis.

CHRIS PERKINS is Reader in Geography at the University of Manchester, where he has taught since 1998, having previously run the university map libraries. His research interests lie at the interface between mapping technologies and social and cultural practices, with ongoing research into performative aspects of contemporary mapping behaviour, an interest in sensory mapping, and an emerging interest in play. He is author of numerous single and co-authored books and academic articles and has listened to *The Archers* for forty-five years. He urges everyone to think about the geography of Ambridge!

KATHERINE RUNSWICK-COLE is Professor of Critical Disability Studies and Psychology at Manchester Metropolitan University. She locates her work in the field of critical disability studies which aims to understand and challenge exclusionary and oppressive practices associated with disablism and to consider the ways these intersect with other forms of marginalization including hetero/sexism, racism, poverty and imperialism. She has published extensively in the field. She was introduced to *The Archers* as an undergraduate student at the University of St Andrews back in the 1980s. She is very excited to be able combine her passion for disability studies with *The Archers*; it is a huge source of enjoyment for her to be part of this exciting book.

LYN THOMAS is part-time Professor of Cultural Studies at the University of Sussex and Emeritus Professor of Cultural Studies at London Metropolitan University. She is author of the online memoir *Clothes Pegs: A Woman's Life in 30 Outfits*. Her book *Fans, Feminisms and 'Quality' Media* (2002) included chapters on *The Archers* and its listeners; more recently she has published a journal article and chapter on online fan cultures around *The Archers*. She thought her work was done, until *Academic Archers* (and Rob Titchener) came along.

SAMANTHA WALTON is Lecturer in English Literature: Writing and the Environment at Bath Spa University. She works on modern and contemporary writing, with particular interest in ecology and psychology in literature. Her book, *Guilty But Insane: Mind and Law in Golden Age Detective Fiction*, was published by Oxford University Press in 2015. She co-edits the journal *Green Letters: Studies in Ecocriticism* and has held Visiting Research Fellowships at the University of Edinburgh and the University of Aberdeen. One day, she hopes to co-author a paper on classical ecology with Professor Jim Lloyd. In the meantime, she'll take a pint of scrumpy.

Index of *Archers* Characters